World's Best ORIGAMI for Kids

Woof!

BEETLE
BOOKS

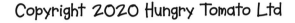

Beetle Books is a Hungry Tomato imprint
First published in 2020 by Hungry Tomato Ltd
F1, Old Bakery Studios
Blewetts Wharf, Malpas Road,
Cornwall, TR1 1QH. UK

A CIP catalogue record for this book is available
from the British Library

ISBN 978-1-913077-20-4

Printed and bound in China

Discover more at
www.mybeetlebooks.com

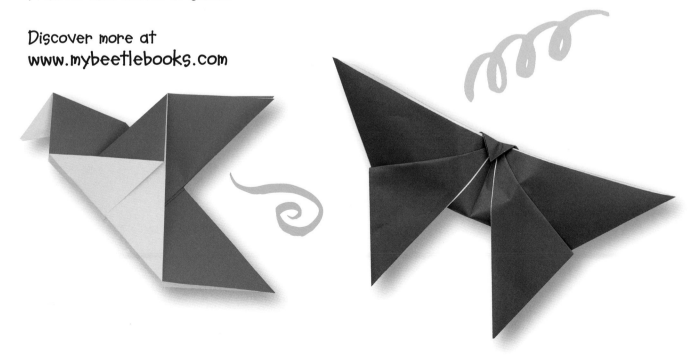

World's Best ORIGAMI for Kids

By Rob Ives

CONTENTS

Origami 8	Plesiosaur 50
Getting started 10	Origami flowers 54
Bird 12	Geometric shapes 58
Butterfly 14	Heart box 62
Fox 16	Square box 66
Dog 18	Talking head 68
Frog 22	Delta-wing plane 70
Mouse 26	Mars lander 74
Rabbit 30	Canoe 78
Dimetrodon 34	Delivery van 81
Allosaurus 36	Classic yacht 84
Ichthyosaur 38	Space rocket 88
Pterosaur 42	Index 92
Iguanodon 46	

ORIGAMI

Origami is the art of paper folding. It began in Japan some time after Buddhist monks brought paper to the country during the 6th century, more than 1,400 years ago. The name is from "ori"—"folding"—and "kami," meaning "paper."

One of the most famous origami designs is the Japanese crane. Legend says that anyone who folds one thousand paper cranes will have their heart's desire come true. We have our own interpretation of this with the bird on page 12.

Origami paper

The only requirement for the paper is that it must hold a crease, and ideally it should be thinner than regular paper. Traditional Japanese origami paper comes in many patterns, colors, and styles, and can often be found in your local craft store or in an online store.

GETTING STARTED

Work on a table or flat surface. It makes it easier to create tight folds.

Make sure the folds are accurate at the points. This is crucial to make sure you have a great-looking finished sculpture.

Make the folds firm. This will help the origami stay in place and give a nice, clean finish.

Woof!

Folds and Arrows

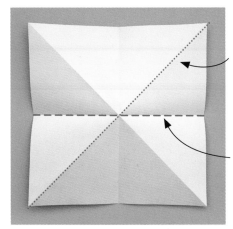

Mountain Fold
Fold the paper along this line **away** from you.

Valley Fold
Fold the paper along this line **toward** you.

If you turn the paper over, a mountain fold becomes a valley fold.

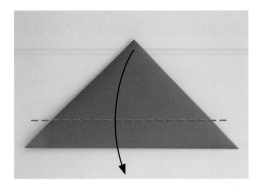

Folding direction
Fold over in this direction.

A dotted line on the arrow means fold to the back or inside.

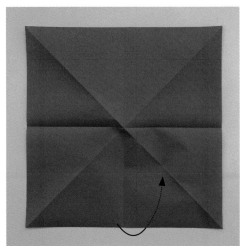

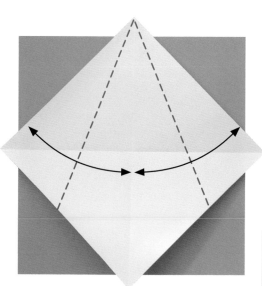

Make a crease
Fold the paper in the direction of the arrow and open it out again.

Open out
This is not as tricky as it looks! Follow the steps below:

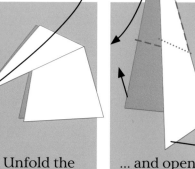

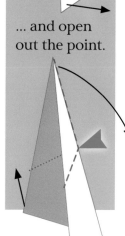

Unfold the crease ...

... and open out the point.

Refold the creases the other way to turn the tip inside (above) or outside (below).

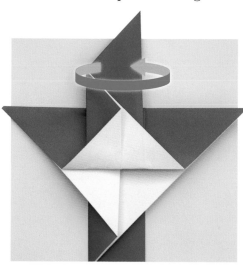

Turn over
Turn the paper over.

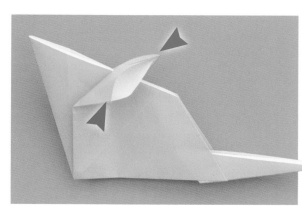

Push
Press in at the points shown.

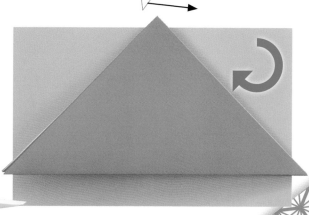

Rotate
Rotate the model as shown.

BIRD

This beautiful bird is a white dove, which has been a sign of peace for thousands of years.

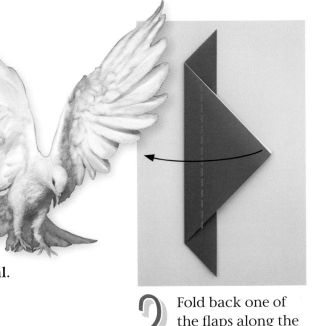

A variation on a traditional origami bird.
Start with a single sheet, folded along a diagonal.

1 Fold both sides back along the vertical crease line.

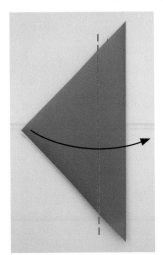

2 Fold back one of the flaps along the marked vertical crease line.

3 Fold the model in half along the horizontal crease line.

4 Fold up one side along the horizontal line.

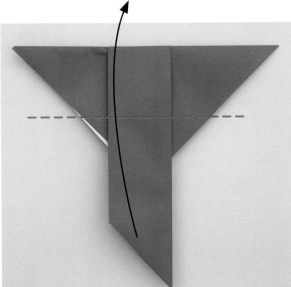

5 Flip the model over.

6 Fold up the other side to match.

7 Fold down along the diagonal line marked. Rotate 45 degrees counterclockwise.

8 Open out the crease and refold, tucked to the inside to create the bird's beak.

BUTTERFLY

Butterflies are the most beautiful of the insects. There are about 17,500 varieties, and they have been on Earth for 55 million years. The largest is Queen Alexandra's birdwing, which lives in New Guinea, and has a wingspan of 10 inches.

Start with a single sheet, face down, and with the diagonals folded.

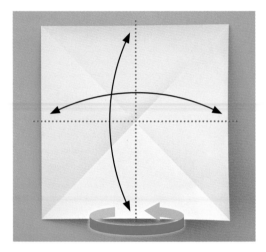

1 Fold and unfold the vertical and horizontal creases, then flip the sheet over.

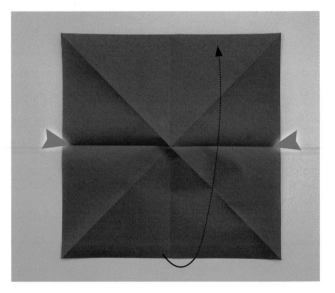

2 Fold the bottom edge back to meet the top edge. As you do so, tuck in the horizontal center crease to make an inverted triangle.

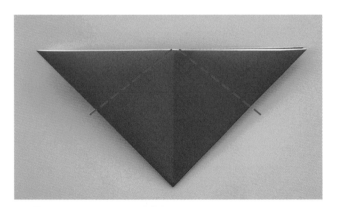

3 Fold down the two front pieces on the crease lines. Note that they are not quite to the center line.

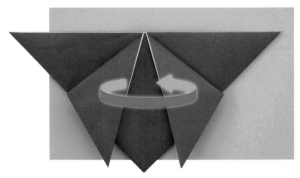

4 Flip the model over.

14

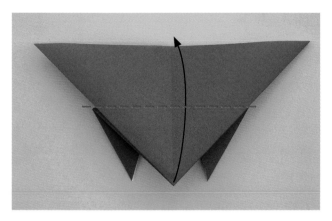

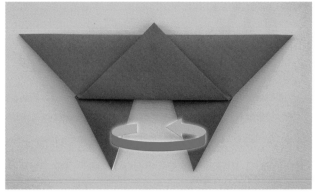

5 Fold up the triangle along the crease line.

6 Flip the model again.

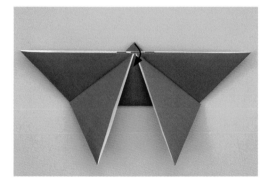

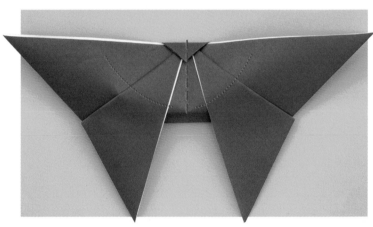

7 Fold over the tip.

8 Fold the butterfly at the vertical crease, and gently fold the wings back to give them shape.

FOX

The red fox is the largest and commonest of 12 fox species spread around the world. Unlike dogs, foxes tend not to live in packs but in small family groups. The two parents often live together for life.

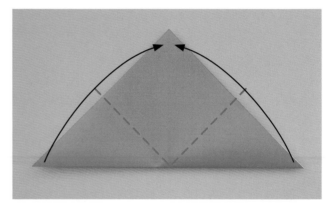

This is a super-simple origami animal! Start with a sheet of paper, face down, at a diagonal, with both diagonals folded.

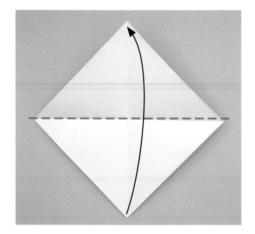

1 Fold up the bottom corner to the top.

2 Fold in the two bottom corners to the top.

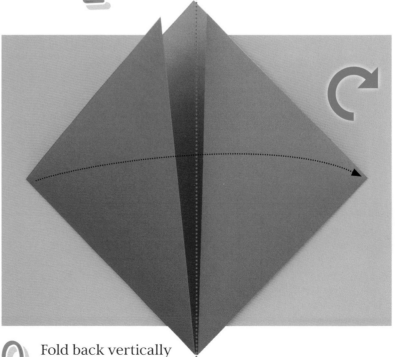

3 Fold back vertically along the center line and rotate 45 degrees clockwise.

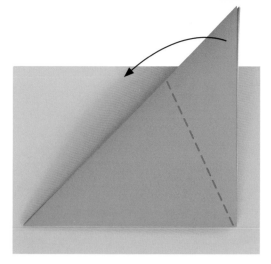

4 Fold the top layer along the marked crease line.

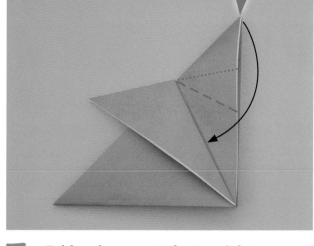

5 Fold and open out the top right flap to make the fox's face.

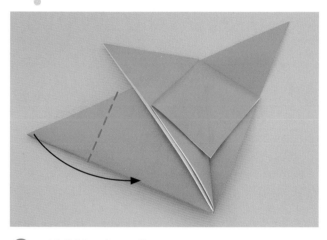

6 Fold in the tail.

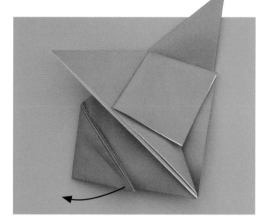

7 Fold the tail out to 90 degrees so that the model stands up. Add a face with a pen.

DOG

This smart little puppy resembles the West Highland terrier, commonly called a "Westie." Originally from Scotland, UK, these little dogs are intelligent, quick to learn, and good with kids.

Start with a sheet of paper, face down, at a diagonal. Pre-crease both diagonals.

1 Fold and unfold all the edges to the diagonal center lines to create this crease pattern.

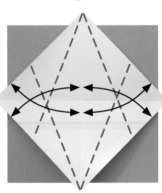

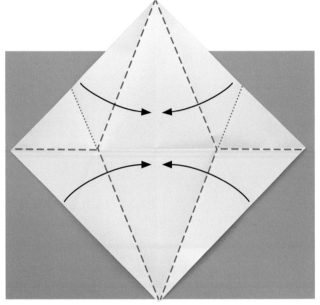

2 Fold in the sides while lifting the left and right corners. Fold flat to make a diamond shape.

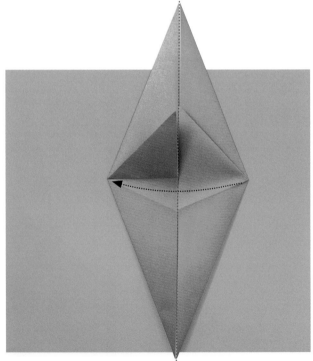

3 Fold back along the center line so that the two ears are on the outside.

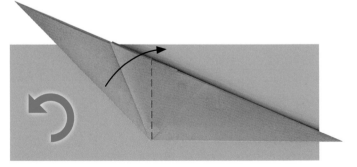

4 Turn the sheet so it looks like this, then fold along the crease line.

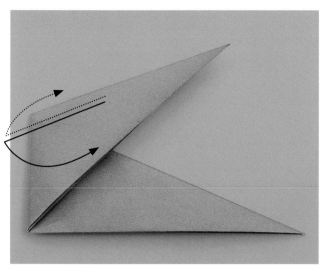 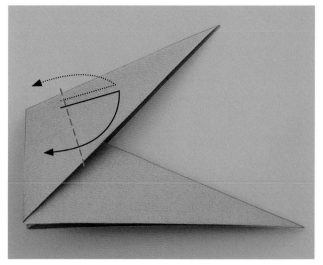

5 Open out to the outside of the model. Fold along the crease line and then open out with the top portion again on the outside of the model. Leave the ears sticking out.

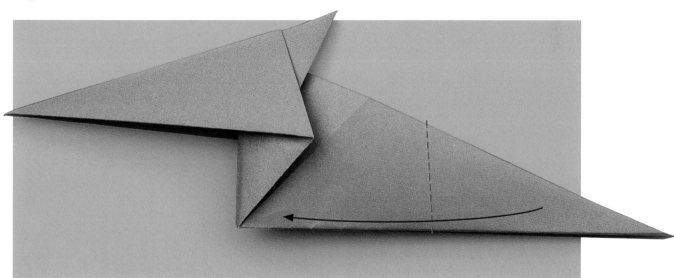

6 Fold over along the crease line.

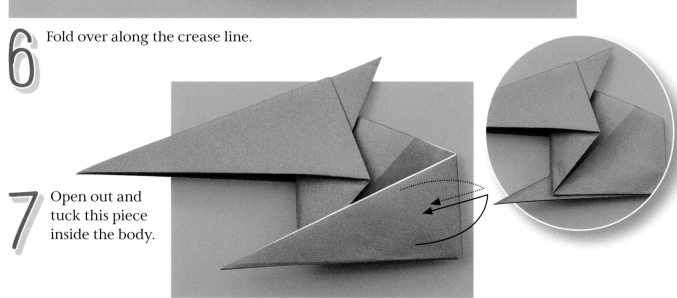

7 Open out and tuck this piece inside the body.

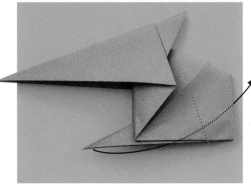

8 Fold the tail back inside, so that it touches the top back of the body.

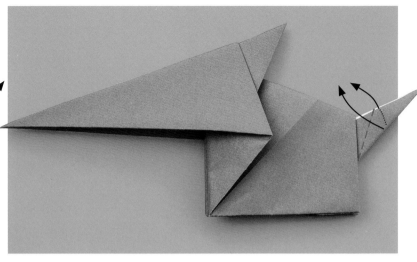

9 Turn the tail inside out along the crease line so that it points straight up.

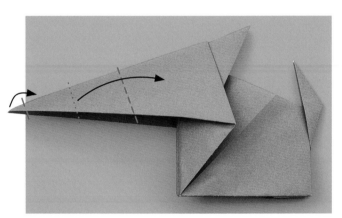

10 Zigzag the head in three folds.

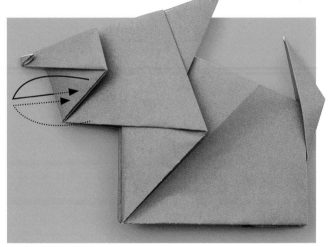

11 Open out and refold the parts inside to tuck the two sections into the head.

12 Fold up the nose by turning it inside out along the crease. Tuck the back of both front legs behind, along the marked crease.

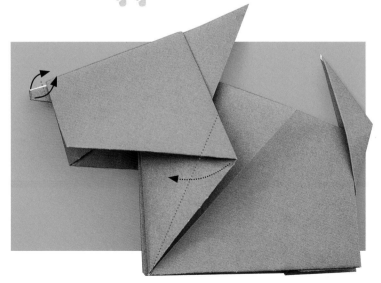

13 To complete the dog, fold the ears forward and shape them out. Push up and shape the underside of the body.

Woof!

FROG

There are almost 7,000 kinds of frog around the world. Many are very colorful. Poison dart frogs are poisonous to protect themselves from predators. The goliath frog is the biggest species, growing up to 7lb. All frogs have an important part to play in our Earth's ecosystem.

This is a traditional origami model. Start with a single sheet, face down, on a diagonal, with horizontal, vertical, and both diagonal creases folded.

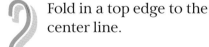

2 Fold in a top edge to the center line.

1 Fold the top corner to the bottom, and at the same time, tuck in the other two corners to make a smaller square.

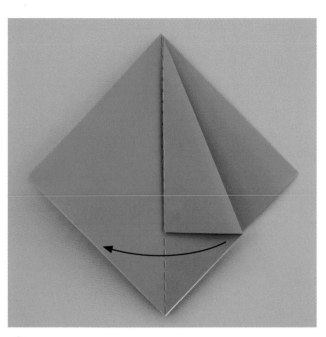

3 Open out the underside of the crease and pull it across to the left edge to make an inverted kite shape.

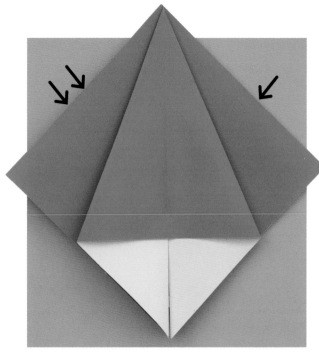

4 Repeat steps 2 and 3 three more times with the other flaps.

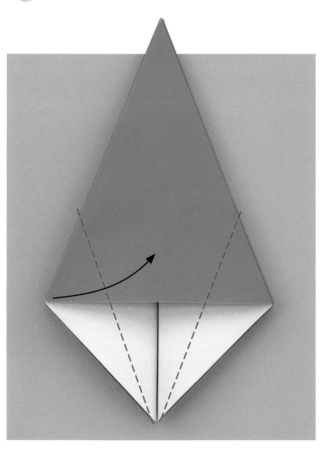

5 Fold up the bottom edges (of the top flap on each side) to the center line.

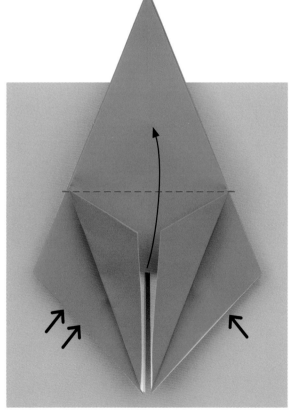

6 Pull up the hidden edge and fold it to the center line, making a kite shape. Repeat steps 5 and 6 on the other three flaps.

7 Fold over the top layer.

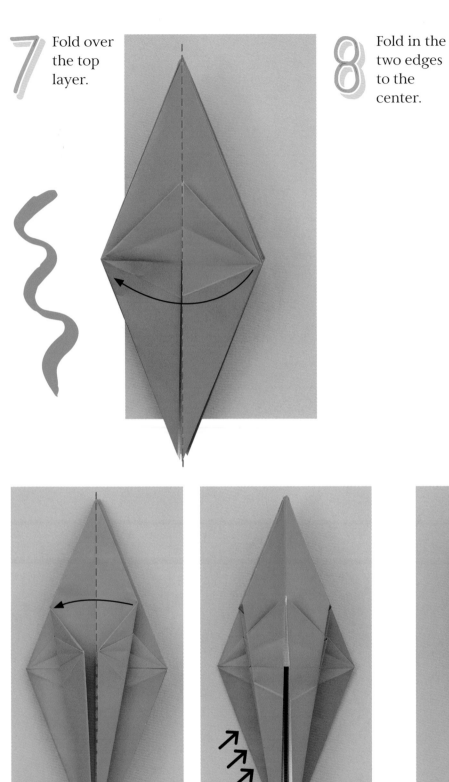

8 Fold in the two edges to the center.

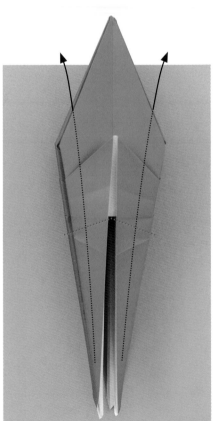

9 Fold the top right flap over to the left. Repeat steps 8 and 9 with the remaining three sides.

10 Crease up the two front legs. Tuck them inside to make the front legs.

11 Crease the bottom legs and tuck them in to make the bottom legs.

12 Fold and tuck the various leg sections to make joints.

13 Blow into the frog to inflate it!

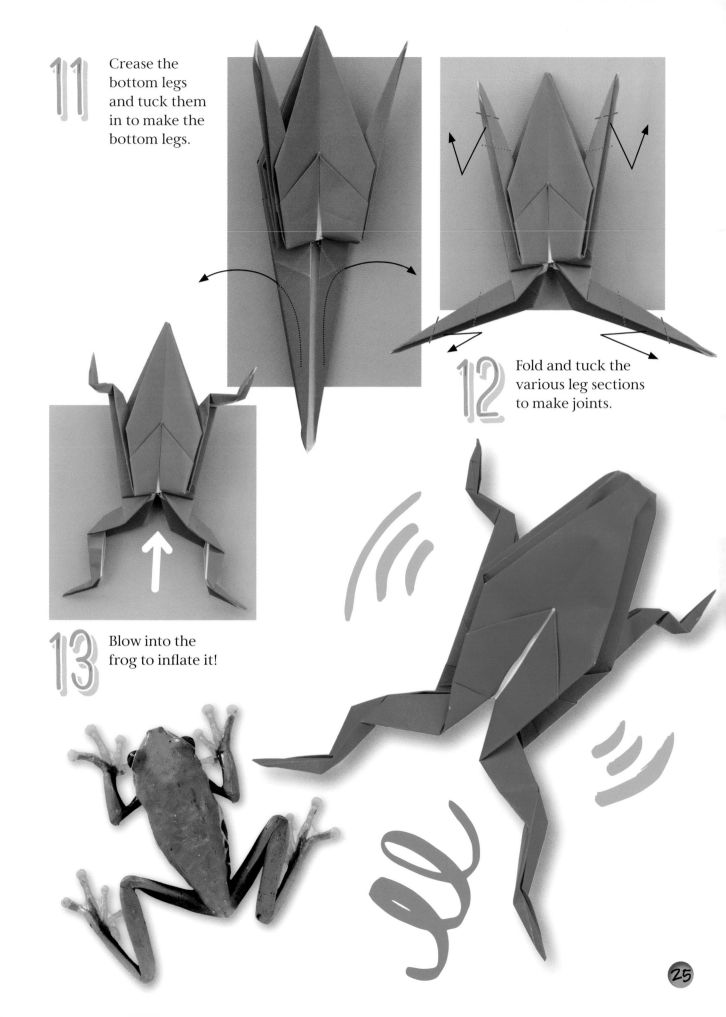

MOUSE

There are many different kinds of mouse, and they live all around us: outside, and sometimes in our homes as pets. Mice thrive in almost any environment—in forests, farmland, meadows, deserts, and even on mountains. They are the most successful mammals living on Earth today.

Start with a single sheet, face down, at a diagonal, with both diagonals already folded.

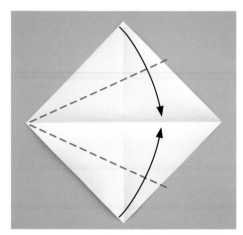

1 Fold in the left side edges to the center line.

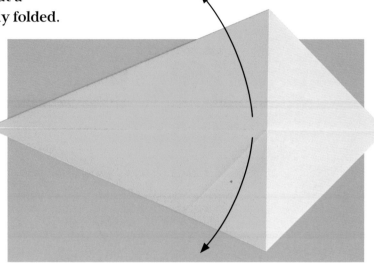

2 Open out the folds.

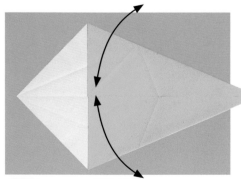

3 Fold in the right side edges to the center line, then unfold.

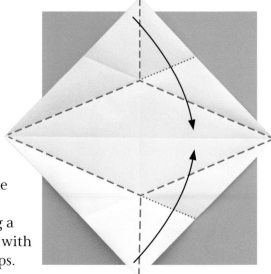

4 Fold in along the newly created creases, making a diamond shape with two triangle flaps.

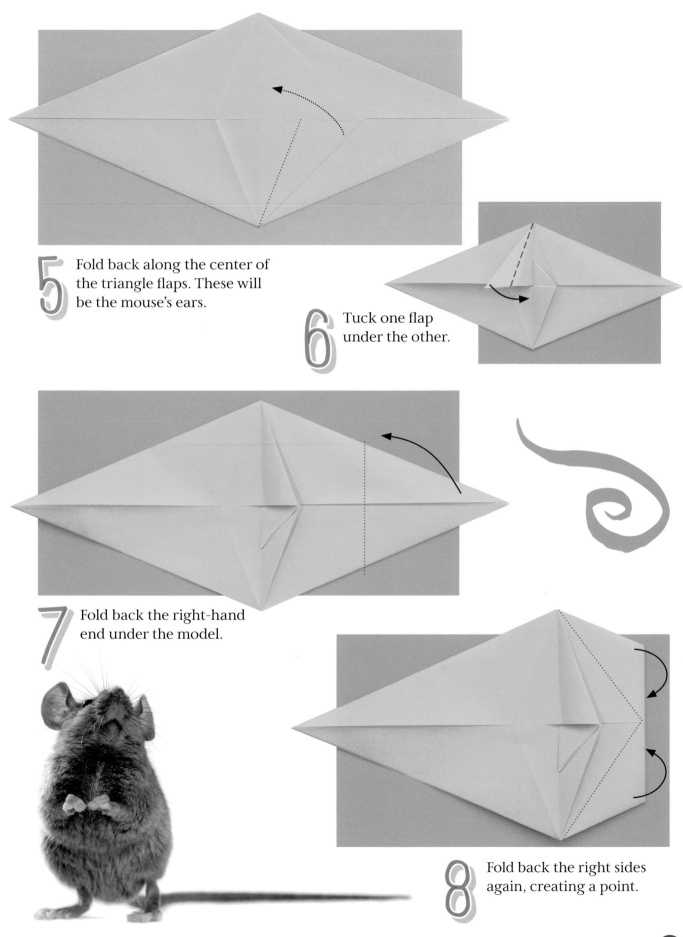

5 Fold back along the center of the triangle flaps. These will be the mouse's ears.

6 Tuck one flap under the other.

7 Fold back the right-hand end under the model.

8 Fold back the right sides again, creating a point.

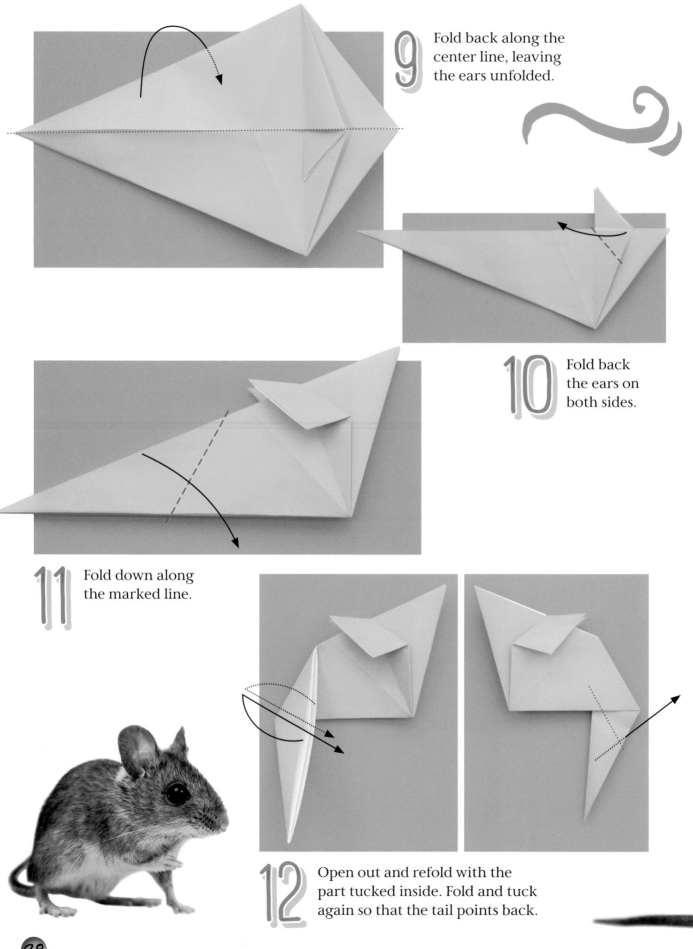

9 Fold back along the center line, leaving the ears unfolded.

10 Fold back the ears on both sides.

11 Fold down along the marked line.

12 Open out and refold with the part tucked inside. Fold and tuck again so that the tail points back.

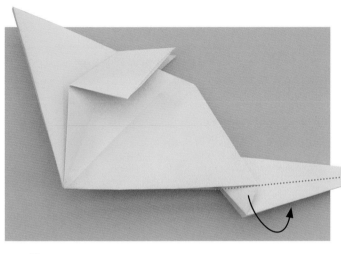

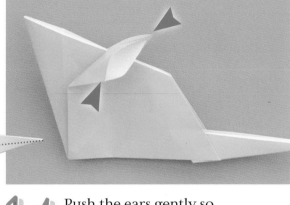

13 Fold the lower parts of the tail up and inside the tail to complete the model.

14 Push the ears gently so they open.

Eek!

RABBIT

In the wild, rabbits live in groups of burrows called warrens. They eat little except grass. If confronted with danger, a rabbit will first freeze and observe. If the danger persists, it will thump the ground with its hind legs to warn other rabbits in the warren.

This is a variation on a traditional origami rabbit. Start with a single sheet, face down, and folded in half along the horizontal center line.

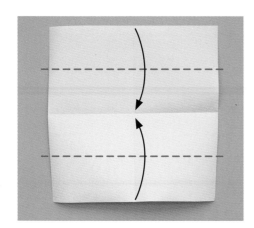

1 Fold the top and bottom edges into the middle.

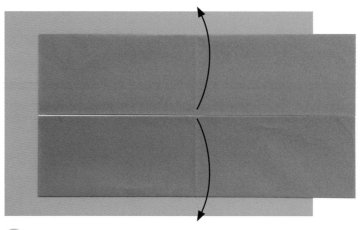

2 Unfold, then fold the right and left edges into the center line.

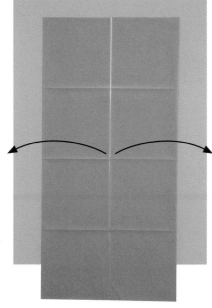

3 Unfold the sheet.

4 Fold the two lower corners to the center and unfold. Fold the two diagonals and unfold.

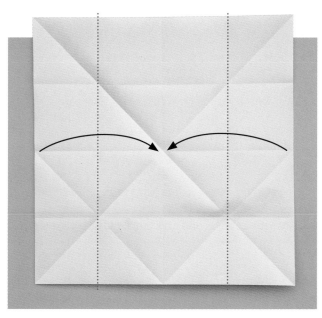

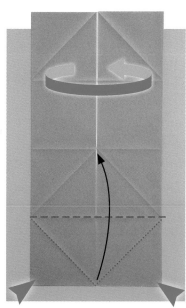

6 Fold up and tuck inside the two bottom triangles. Then flip the sheet over.

5 Fold back the right and left sides into the center.

8 Fold along the crease line shown, allowing the hidden flap underneath to fold forward. Fold the bottom tip back (see step 9 for the result).

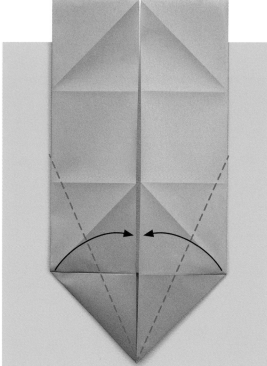

7 Fold the lower edges to the center.

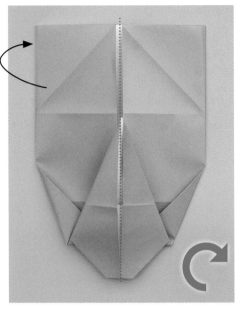

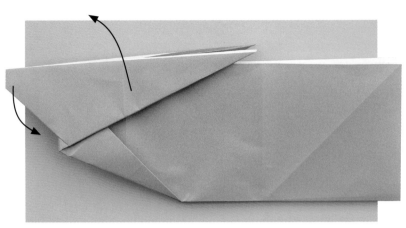

9 Fold in half along the vertical crease line. Rotate 90 degrees clockwise.

10 Grasp the lower part of the two ears and lift them free of the body, rotating the head down as you do so. Press the model flat.

11 Fold the back of the model forward along the crease line.

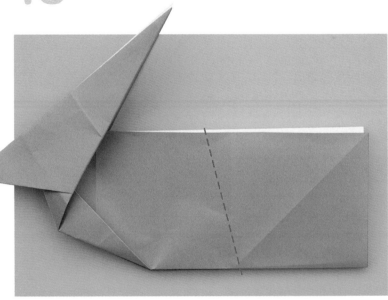

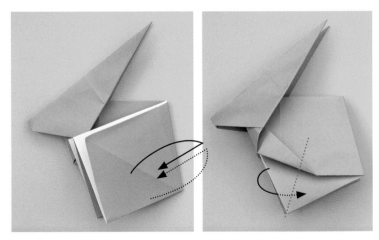

12 Unfold then refold with the parts tucked inside. Fold back along the crease lines to create the legs.

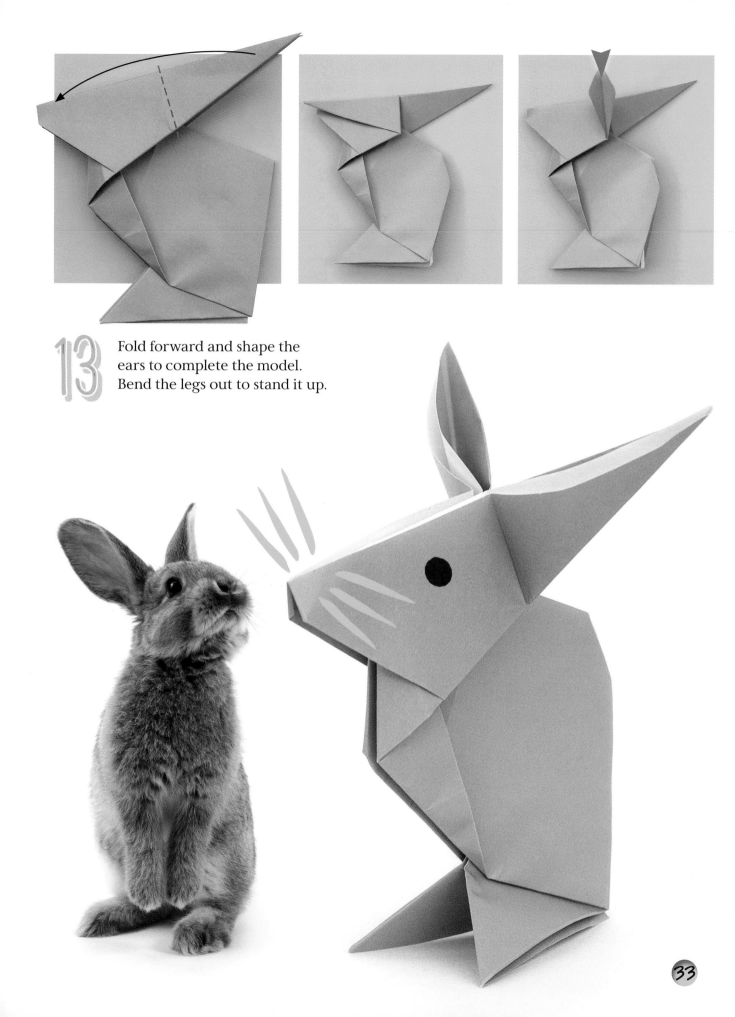

13 Fold forward and shape the ears to complete the model. Bend the legs out to stand it up.

DIMETRODON

This strange-looking animal died out 40 million years before the first dinosaurs roamed Earth. It may have used the enormous spiny sail on its back in courtship displays.

Start with a sheet of paper, color side down. Fold both diagonals, as well as the vertical and horizontal centers.

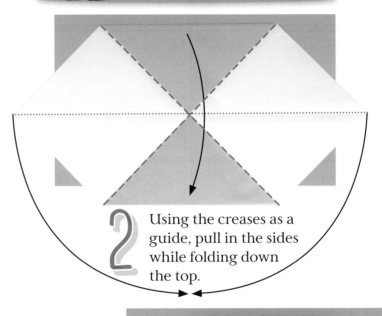

1 Fold up the top and bottom into the center.

2 Using the creases as a guide, pull in the sides while folding down the top.

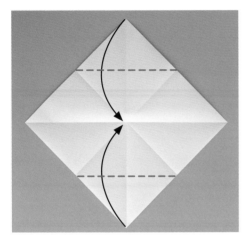

3 Fold the top point down to the center.

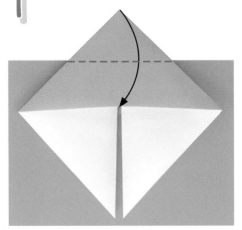

4 Fold in the sides about one third of the way.

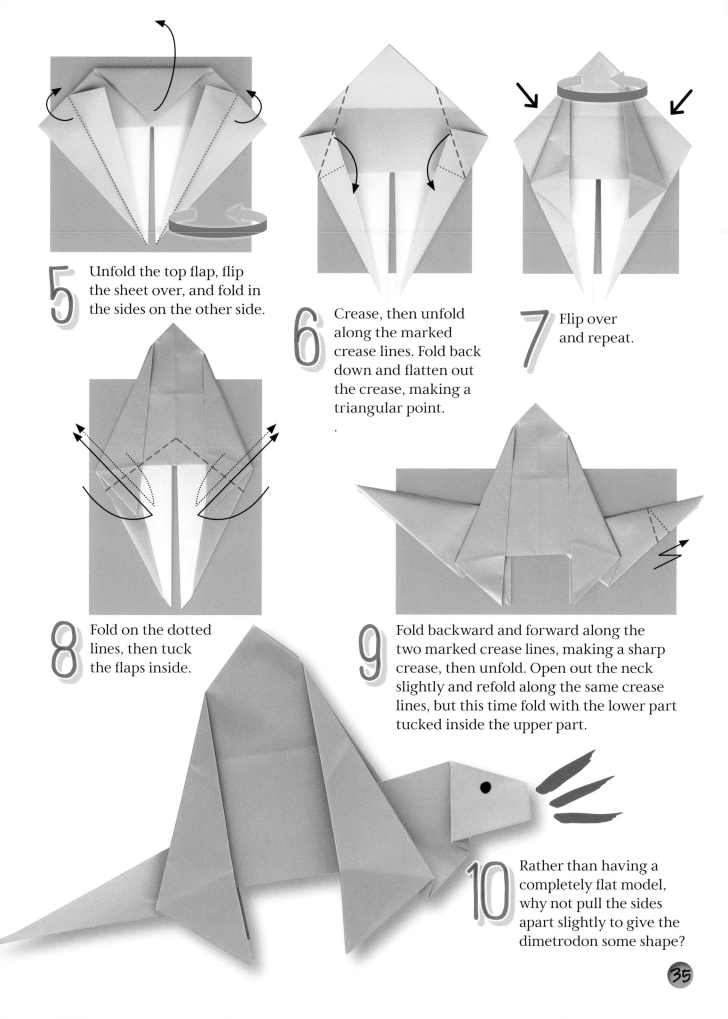

5 Unfold the top flap, flip the sheet over, and fold in the sides on the other side.

6 Crease, then unfold along the marked crease lines. Fold back down and flatten out the crease, making a triangular point.

7 Flip over and repeat.

8 Fold on the dotted lines, then tuck the flaps inside.

9 Fold backward and forward along the two marked crease lines, making a sharp crease, then unfold. Open out the neck slightly and refold along the same crease lines, but this time fold with the lower part tucked inside the upper part.

10 Rather than having a completely flat model, why not pull the sides apart slightly to give the dimetrodon some shape?

ALLOSAURUS

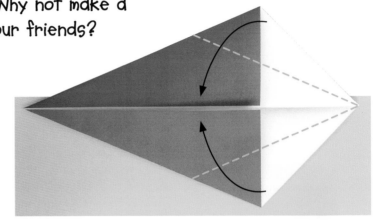

Allosaurus had large jaws with dozens of sharp, serrated teeth. This giant dinosaur was definitely at the top of the food chain. Why not make a scary dinosaur head to wow your friends?

Start with a sheet of paper, color side down.

1 First, fold along a diagonal, then fold in the sides to make a kite shape. Fold in along the dotted lines.

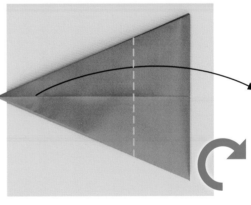

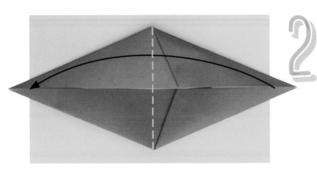

2 Fold in half along the dotted line.

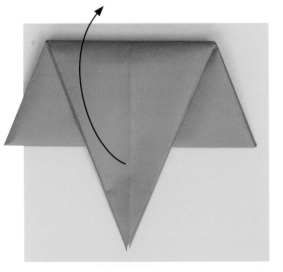

3 Fold both layers along the dotted line. Rotate 90 degrees clockwise.

4 Open out the top layer by unfolding the previous fold.

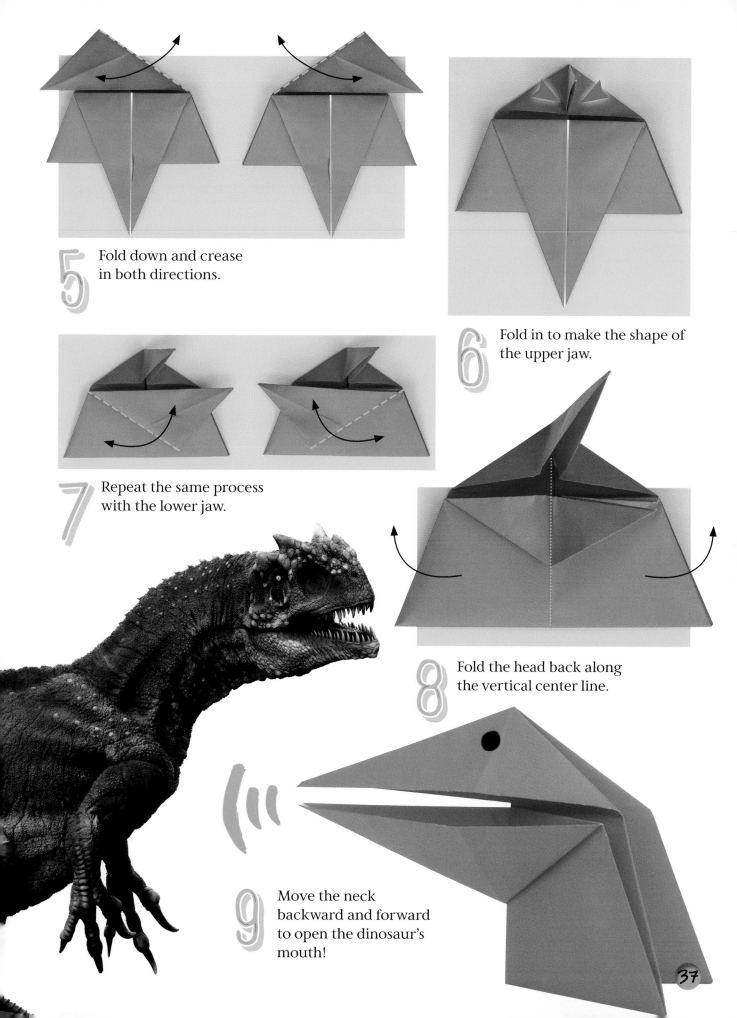

5 Fold down and crease in both directions.

6 Fold in to make the shape of the upper jaw.

7 Repeat the same process with the lower jaw.

8 Fold the head back along the vertical center line.

9 Move the neck backward and forward to open the dinosaur's mouth!

ICHTHYOSAUR

This very large marine reptile swam through our oceans for more than 160 million years. It hunted fish in the open ocean as well as in coastal waters.

For your very own ichthyosaur, start with a sheet of paper, color side down. Fold along a diagonal line.

1 First fold in two sides to the center. Then fold back along the center line.

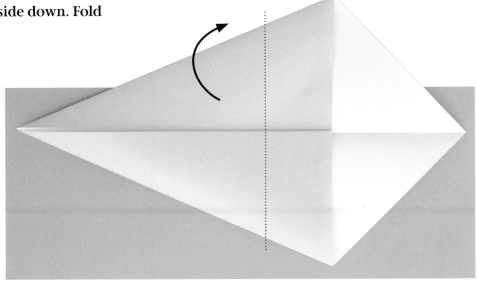

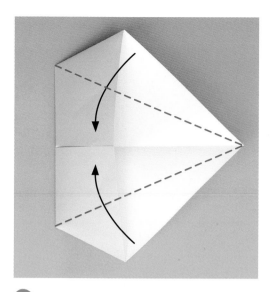

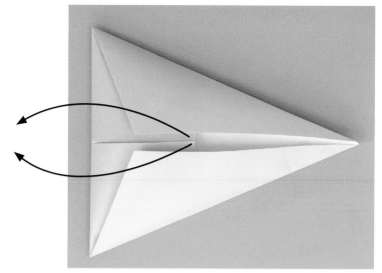

 Fold the sides down along the dotted lines so the edges meet the center line.

 Pull out and flatten to make a kite shape.

 Unfold out from underneath. Then flip over.

 Double fold backward and forward.

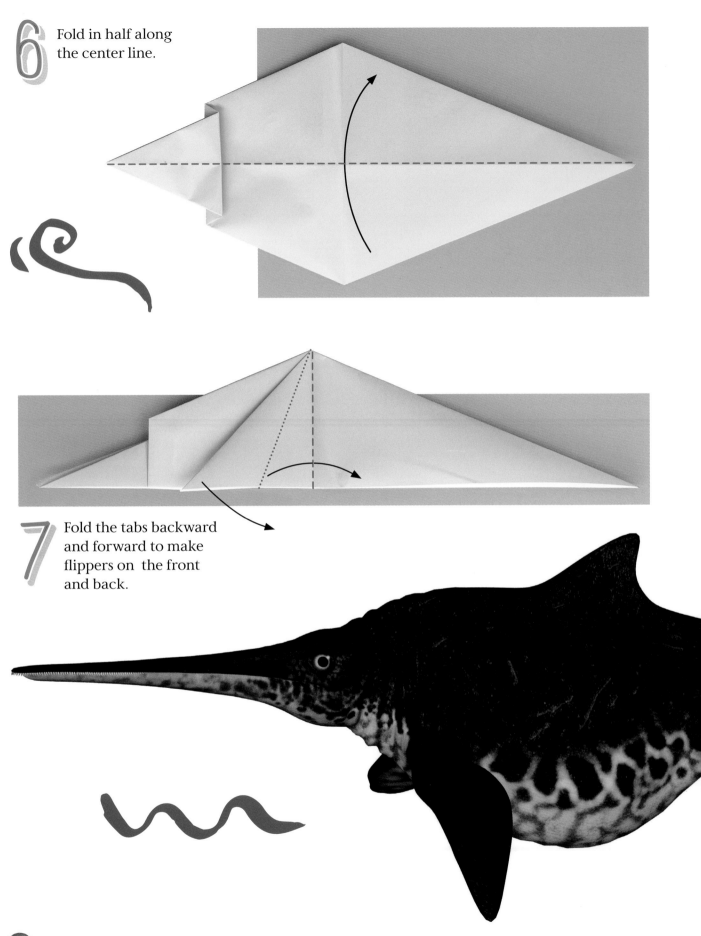

6 Fold in half along the center line.

7 Fold the tabs backward and forward to make flippers on the front and back.

8 Fold up along the crease line.

9 Unfold and refold the tail with the tail fin on the inside to complete the ichthyosaur.

PTEROSAUR

Pterosaurs were long–winged reptiles that were capable of powered flight. These amazing creatures survived for 150 million years, pursuing and catching large flying bugs in their huge jaws, packed with sharp teeth. Some pterosaurs could also swim.

For your own flying reptile, start with the sheet color side down. Crease the two diagonal lines.

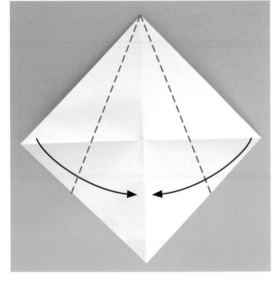

1 Fold in the two sides to the middle.

2 Fold in the sides from the other end. At the same time, pull out the flaps from underneath to make triangle shapes.

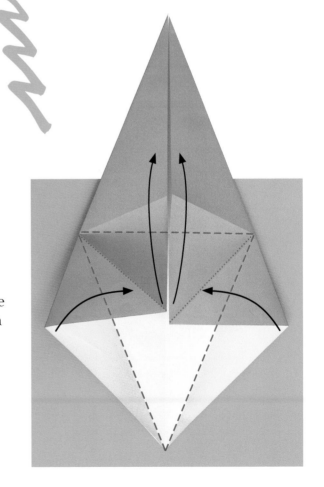

3 Fold the sheet in half.

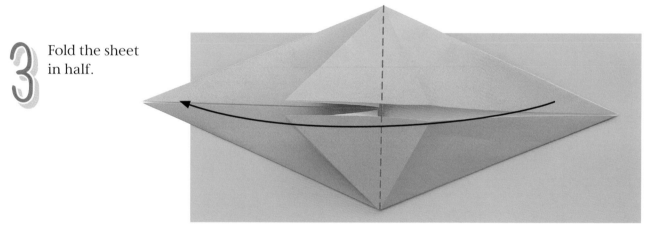

4 Open out the two layers slightly. Reach between the layers and pull the lower inside flaps right out, while folding the layers back together again.

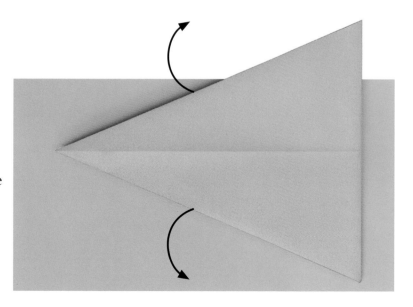

5 Fold the model in half along the horizontal line.

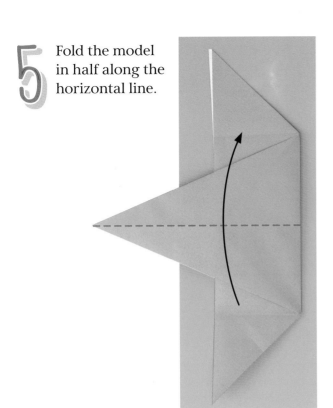

6 Fold up the thin triangle as shown.

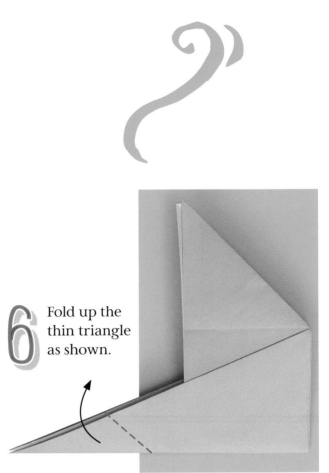

7 Tuck the triangle inside.

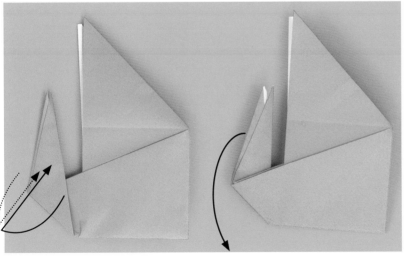

8 Pull back the inner triangle to make a beak. Fold up a section of the body and rotate 90 degrees clockwise.

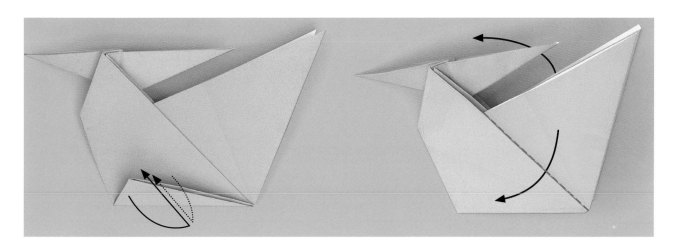

9 Tuck the body section inside. Fold around and shape the wings to complete your pterosaur.

IGUANODON

This plant—eating dinosaur grazed the plains of Europe and Africa 125 million years ago. It was a bulky animal, up to 33 feet long, and it could stand on two legs or four.

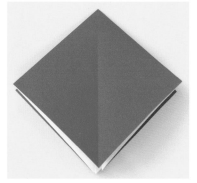

To make your own origami iguanodon:

1 Fold the paper in half along both diagonals, with the white on the outside. Open up the paper.

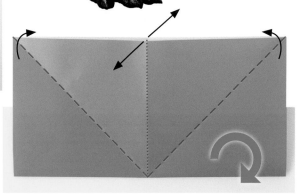

2 Turn the paper over and fold it in half along the horizontal and vertical lines. Pull the two middle parts away from each other and lift the corners up to meet each other.

3 Fold everything down to make a half-size square.

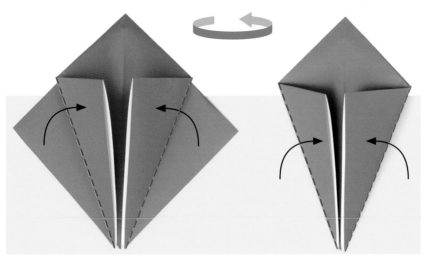

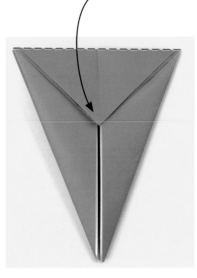

 With the closed corner at the top, fold in the edges to meet the center line. Flip over and repeat.

 Fold over the top and crease along the edge.

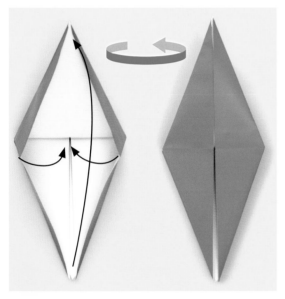

 Lift up the bottom center using the newly created crease line. Pull in the sides and fold everything flat. Flip over and repeat.

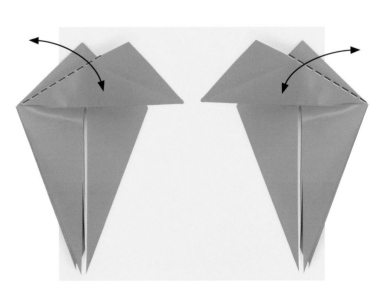

Fold down the top layer along the center fold. Flip over.

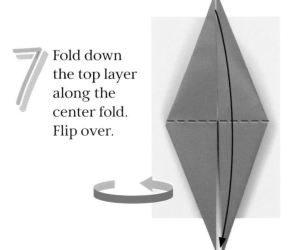

 Fold across, lining up the edge with the horizontal crease line. Crease up to the center. Repeat from the other side.

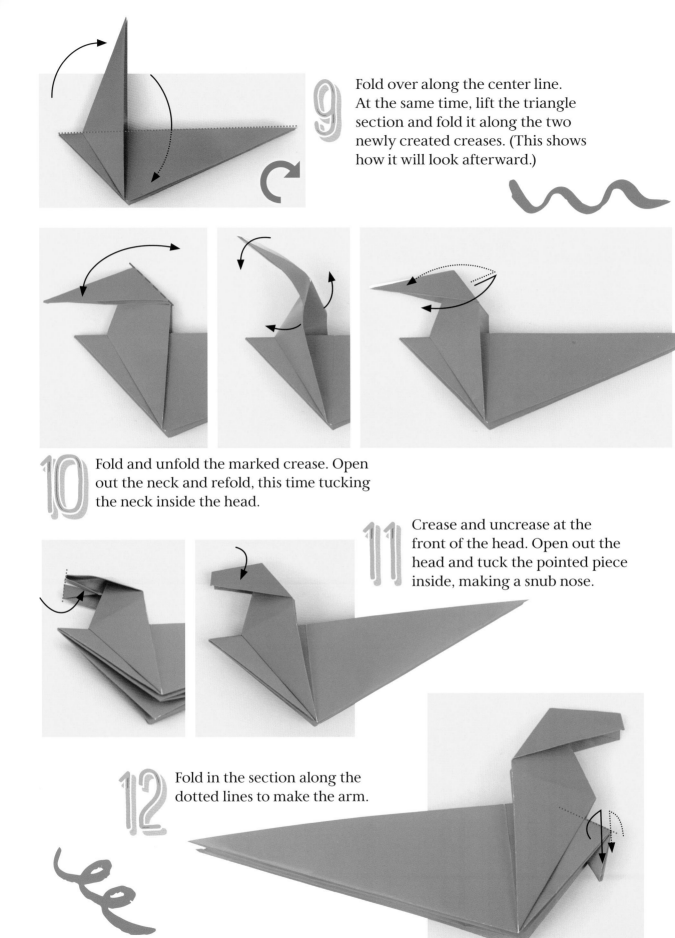

9 Fold over along the center line. At the same time, lift the triangle section and fold it along the two newly created creases. (This shows how it will look afterward.)

10 Fold and unfold the marked crease. Open out the neck and refold, this time tucking the neck inside the head.

11 Crease and uncrease at the front of the head. Open out the head and tuck the pointed piece inside, making a snub nose.

12 Fold in the section along the dotted lines to make the arm.

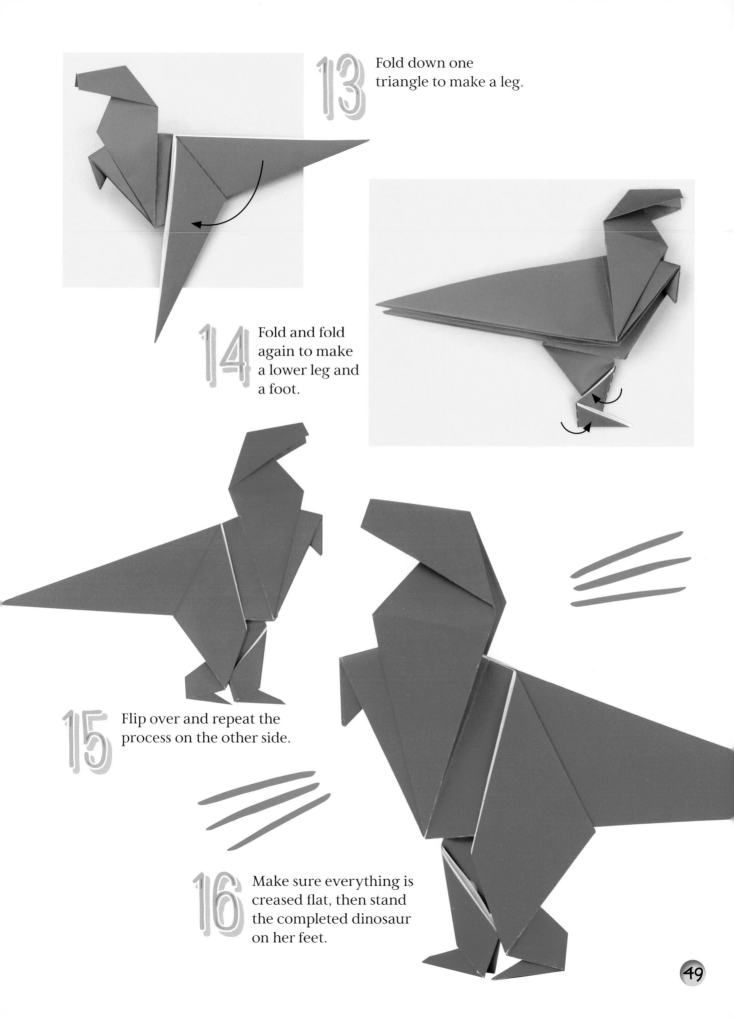

13 Fold down one triangle to make a leg.

14 Fold and fold again to make a lower leg and a foot.

15 Flip over and repeat the process on the other side.

16 Make sure everything is creased flat, then stand the completed dinosaur on her feet.

PLESIOSAUR

This long—necked marine reptile was one of the largest animals ever to have swum in our oceans. It was an apex predator, growing up to 50 feet long, and hunting fish.

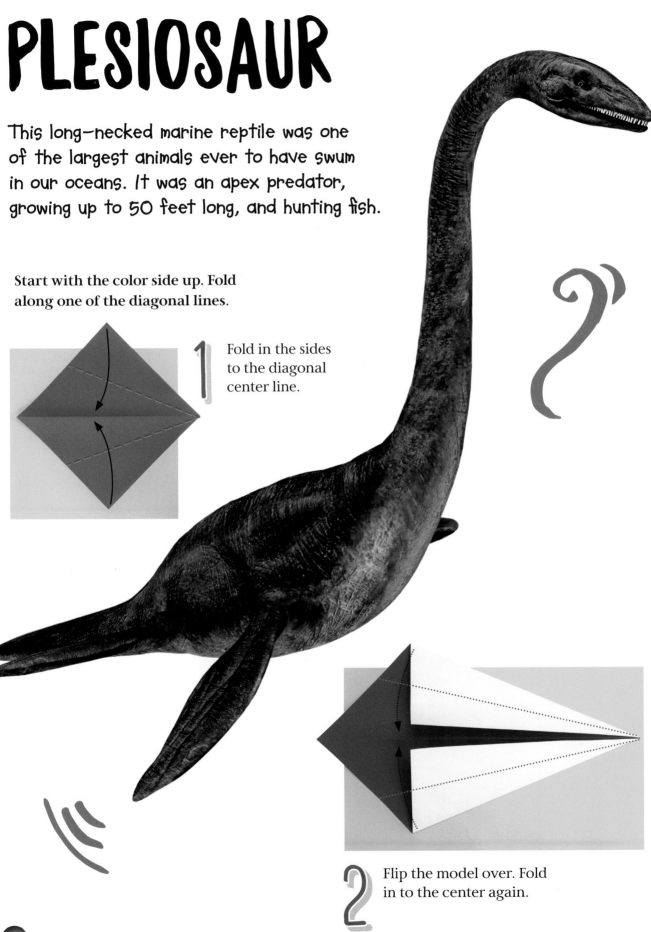

Start with the color side up. Fold along one of the diagonal lines.

1 Fold in the sides to the diagonal center line.

2 Flip the model over. Fold in to the center again.

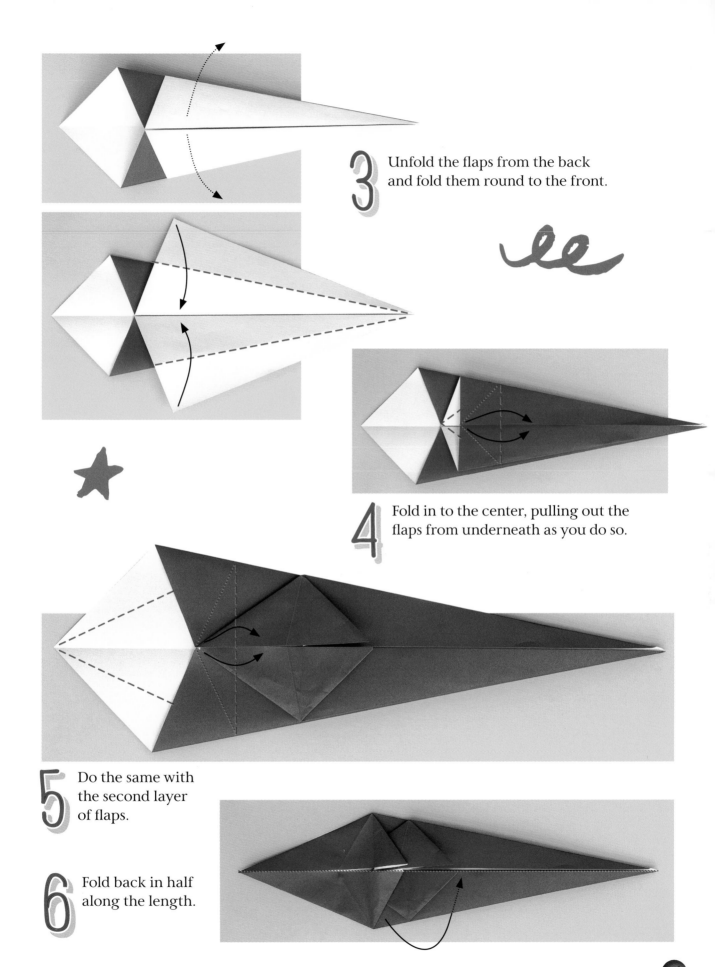

3 Unfold the flaps from the back and fold them round to the front.

4 Fold in to the center, pulling out the flaps from underneath as you do so.

5 Do the same with the second layer of flaps.

6 Fold back in half along the length.

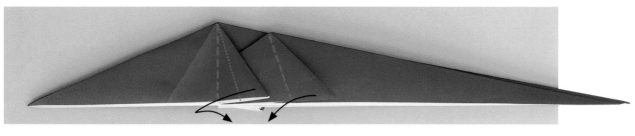

7 Fold down the legs on both sides, along the fold lines.

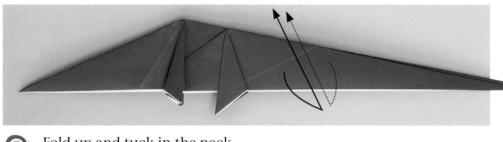

8 Fold up and tuck in the neck.

9 Make two folds along the two dotted lines to make the head.

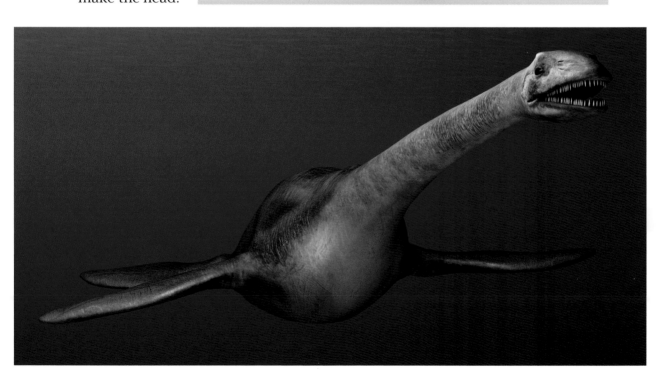

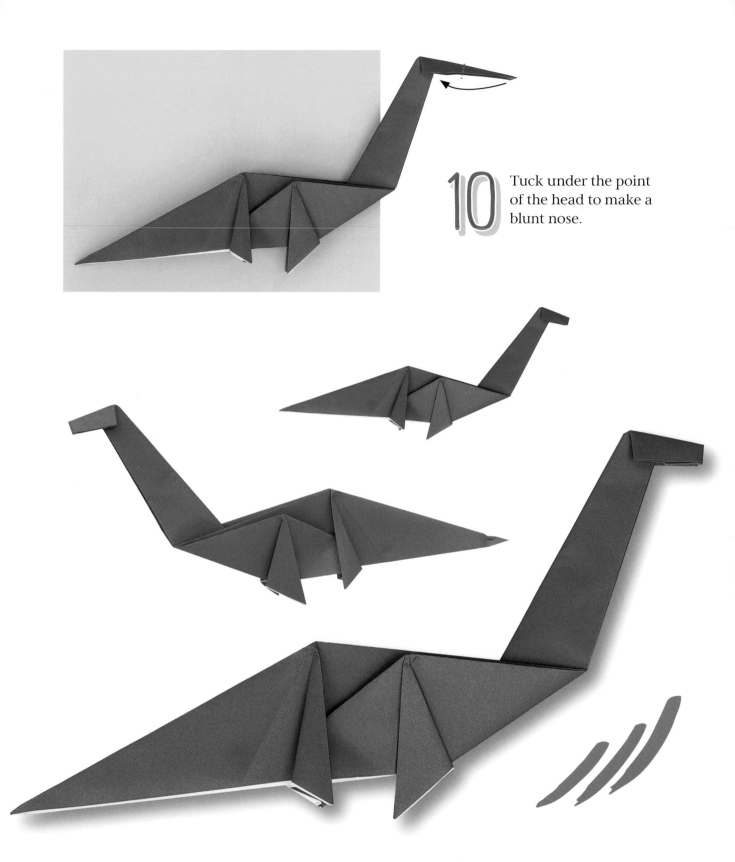

10 Tuck under the point of the head to make a blunt nose.

11 Pull the sides apart a little to pose your model.

ORIGAMI FLOWERS

Flowers are a great gift for your entire family, and what better than one that will never wilt? This origami gift strongly resembles a daffodil, which is often associated with creativity, forgiveness, and the coming of spring.

Start with a sheet folded in half both ways and along the diagonals.

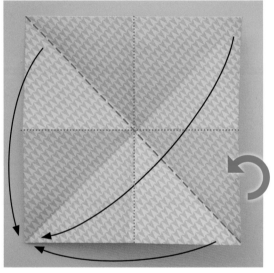

 Fold all the corners in to make a smaller square. Rotate the square 45 degrees so that the open end is at the bottom.

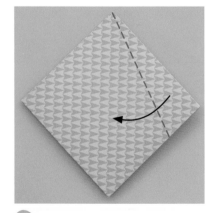

2 Fold the top right side in to the vertical center line.

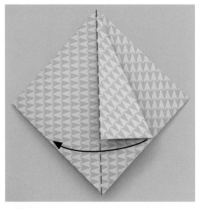

3 Open out the fold to make an inverted kite shape.

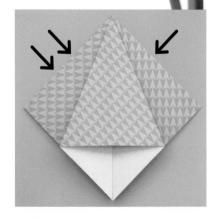

4 Repeat steps 2 and 3 on the other three parts.

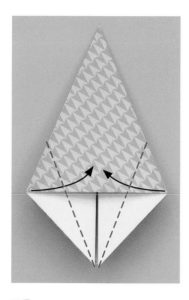

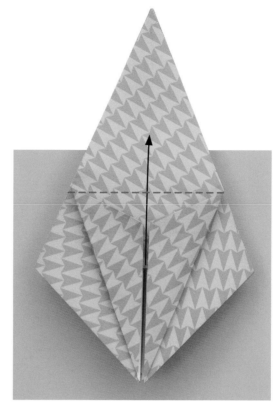

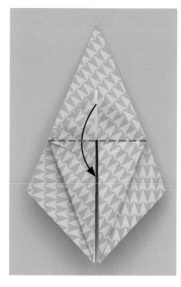

5 Fold up the bottom edges to the center line.

7 Fold down the top of the kite.

6 Lift the two newly created flaps. Grasp the center of the newly revealed horizontal flap and pull it upward, while folding back down the two side flaps. This fold will create the kite shape seen in the next step.

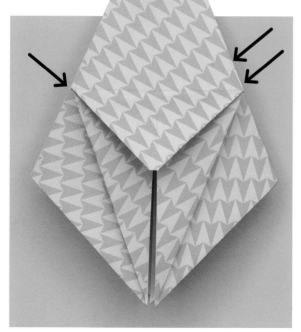

8 Repeat steps 6 and 7 on the other three sides.

9 Rotate the model 180 degrees.

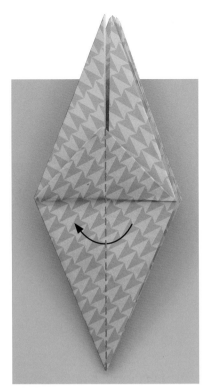

10 Fold the leaf over.

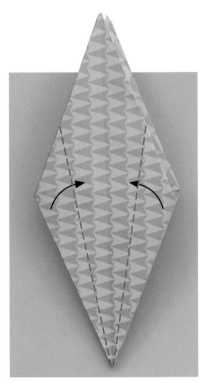

11 Fold in the two lower edges.

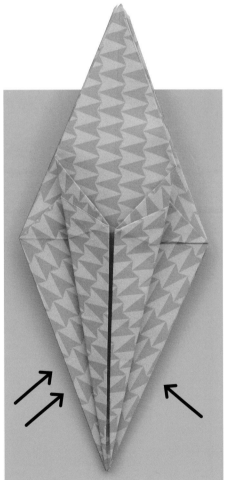

12 Repeat the folds from steps 10 and 11 around the model.

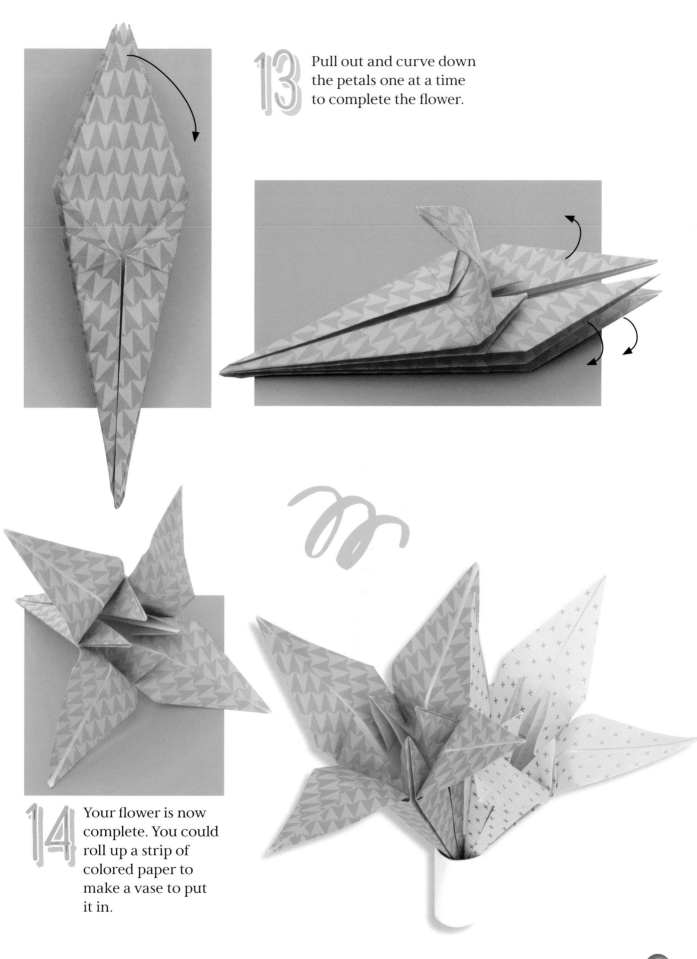

13 Pull out and curve down the petals one at a time to complete the flower.

14 Your flower is now complete. You could roll up a strip of colored paper to make a vase to put it in.

GEOMETRIC SHAPES

This intriguing shape strongly resembles one of the most famous geometric puzzles of all time—the Rubik's cube. Invented in 1974, the puzzle still delights and frustrates people all over the world.

It helps with this model if you use different colored origami papers. Start with a single fold across the horizontal center.

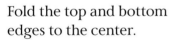

1 Fold the top and bottom edges to the center.

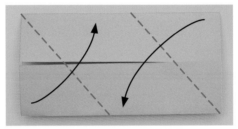

2 Fold the right-hand edge down and the left-hand edge up.

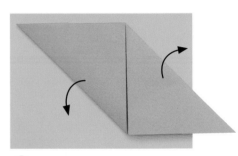

3 Open the sheet out completely.

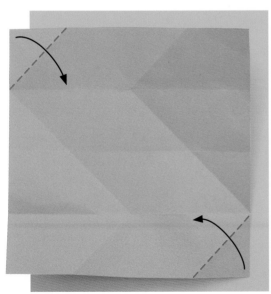

4 Fold in the top left and bottom right triangles.

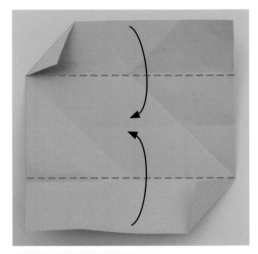

5 Fold the top and bottom edges to the center.

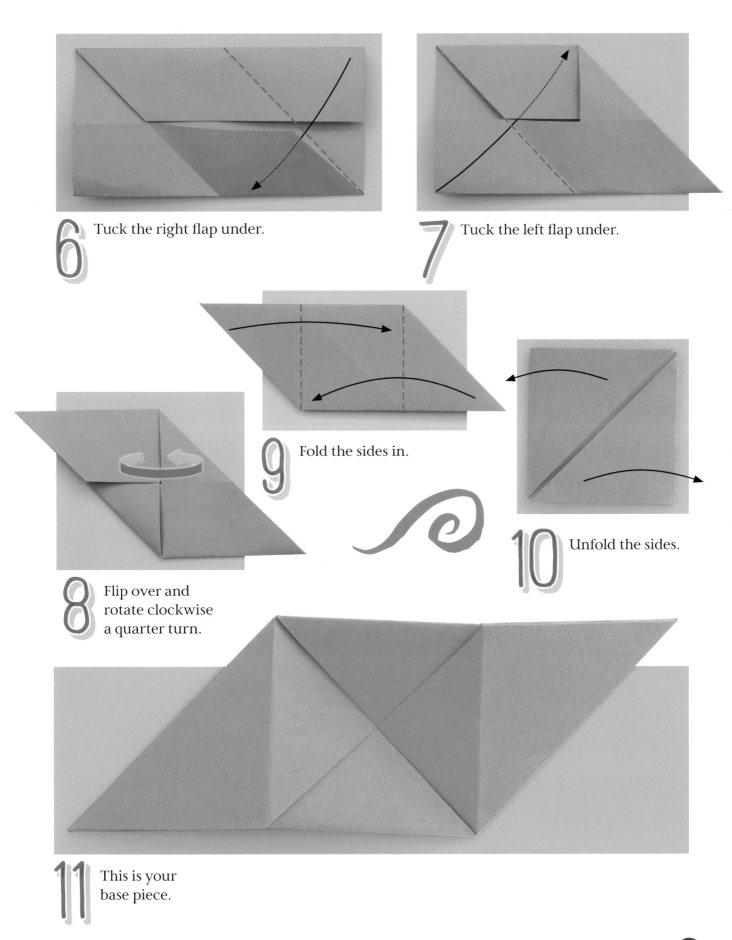

6 Tuck the right flap under.

7 Tuck the left flap under.

9 Fold the sides in.

8 Flip over and rotate clockwise a quarter turn.

10 Unfold the sides.

11 This is your base piece.

12 Make several in different colors.

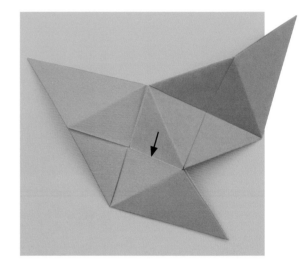

13 Link them together to make geometric shapes.

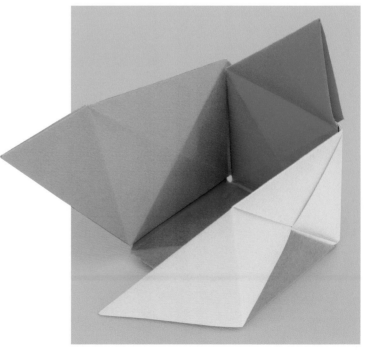

HEART BOX

A heart box is a great way to give a loved one a beautiful gift. Some tasty candy, home-made jewelry or any small gift will be treasured that much more when they are received in a gorgeous package.

Start with a sheet of paper, pattern side down, with the diagonals folded.

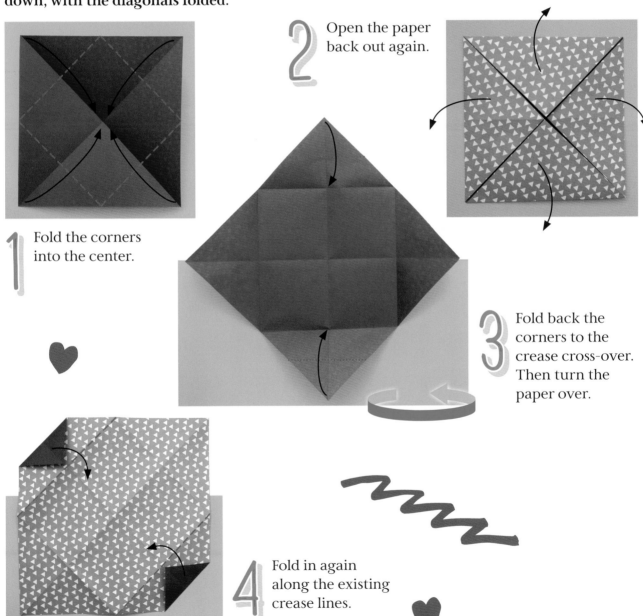

1 Fold the corners into the center.

2 Open the paper back out again.

3 Fold back the corners to the crease cross-over. Then turn the paper over.

4 Fold in again along the existing crease lines.

5 Fold in again to the center.

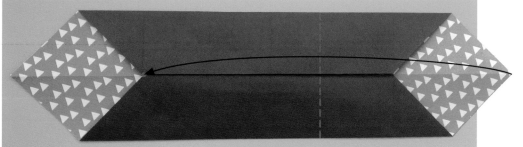

6 Fold the end to the corner marked.

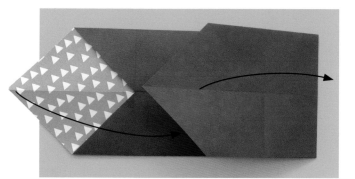

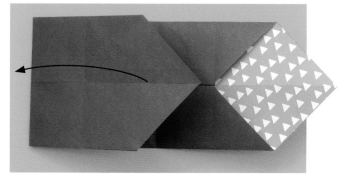

7 Open back out and repeat from the other end.

8 Open out again.

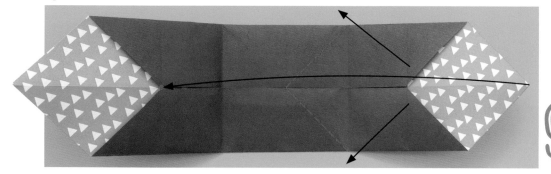

9 Splay out and fold down from the right-hand side.

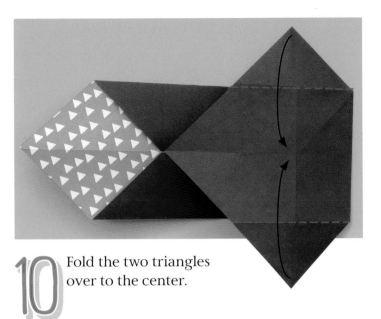

10 Fold the two triangles over to the center.

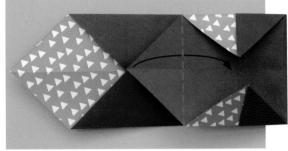

11 Fold the end triangle back.

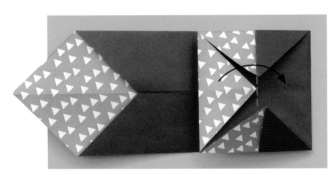

12 Fold over the end.

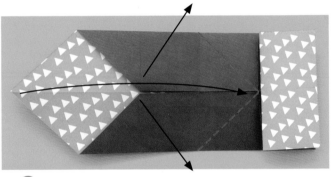

13 Repeat steps 10 to 13 from the other end.

14 Fold the flaps back at the crease lines and tuck them underneath.

15 Tuck a smaller flap underneath at the top.

16 Fold back along the dotted lines, and tuck the flaps back to complete the heart shape.

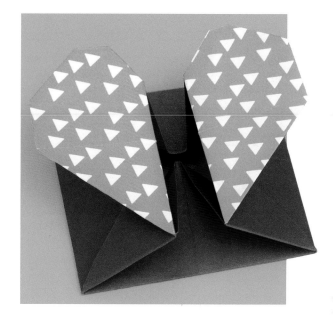

17 Open out the box. Add a message to your true love inside!

SQUARE BOX

This traditional origami design is perfect for holding little treats, a great way to hand out favors to friends at your birthday party—or any other special occasion.

Start with a single sheet, face down, with the vertical and horizontal creases folded.

1 Fold the corners into the center.

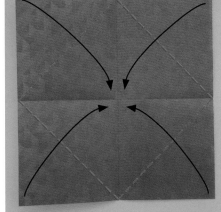

2 Fold and unfold all four edges into the center.

3 Open out the two side triangles.

4 Fold up the sides.

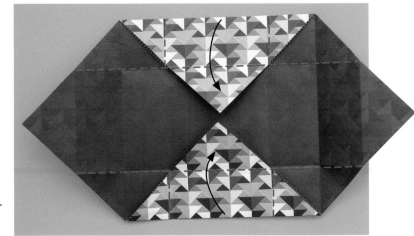

Fold over the left-hand end to the center, and as you do so, trap the triangle sections in place under the flaps.

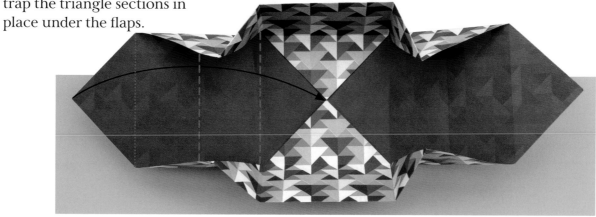

 Repeat the same process from the other end.

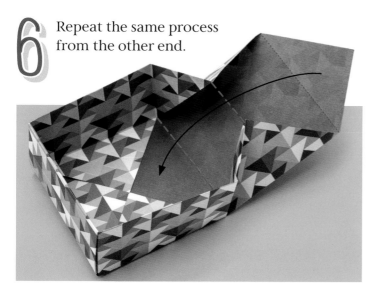

7 Complete the box.

8 To make a small box with a lid, make a second box from a slightly smaller square.

TALKING HEAD

This is another traditional design, and a nice easy model to make. Sometimes called a snapper, it can be used as a puppet—especially if you draw some eyes on it. Make two in different colors and create your own puppet show.

Start with a single sheet, face down, with the vertical and horizontal creases folded.

1 Fold the top and bottom edge to the center.

2 Fold the right-hand edge and left-hand edge up to the top.

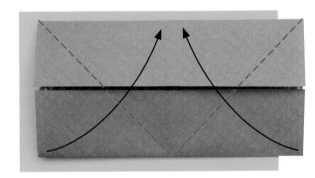

4 Repeat step 2, but fold the other way.

3 Unfold the new creases.

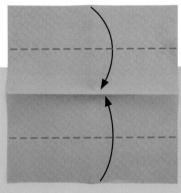

5 Unfold the model again.

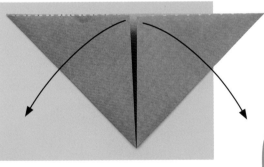

6 Fold the side in to make a triangle.

7 Tuck the flaps one under another.

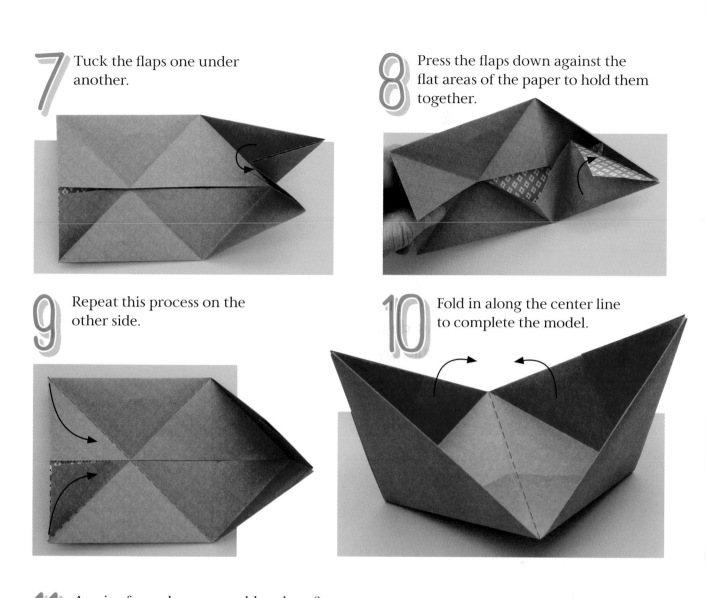

8 Press the flaps down against the flat areas of the paper to hold them together.

9 Repeat this process on the other side.

10 Fold in along the center line to complete the model.

11 A pair of googly eyes would make a fine addition to this simple origami model!

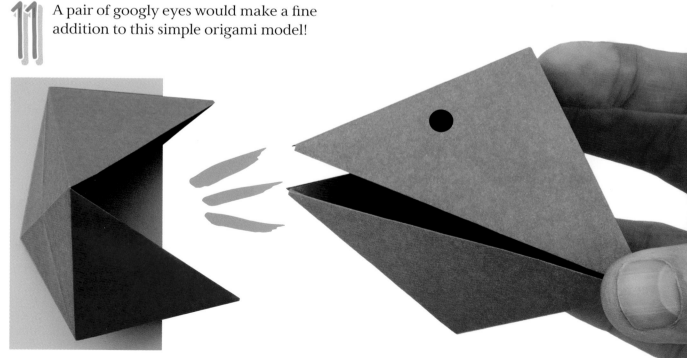

DELTA-WING PLANE

Although delta-wing planes were first developed after WW2, they are the future for supersonic and hypersonic flight. These planes have swept-back wings and no tail. Most superfast jets use this design. Concorde first flew in the 1960s. It could fly faster than the speed of sound to carry passengers across continents and oceans.

Start with a sheet of paper, face down, with the two diagonals folded and the sheet placed at 45 degrees.

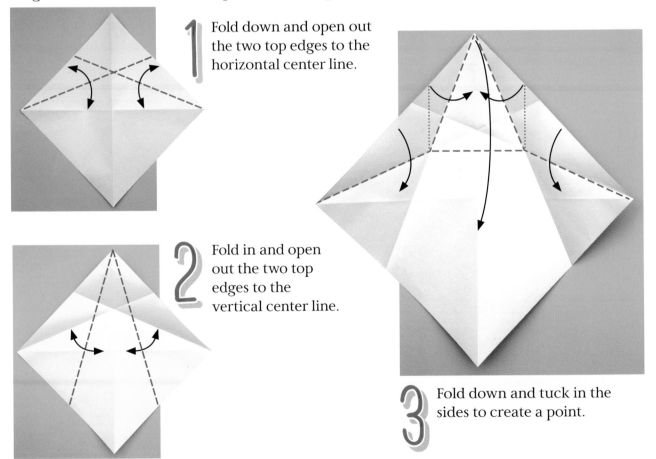

1 Fold down and open out the two top edges to the horizontal center line.

2 Fold in and open out the two top edges to the vertical center line.

3 Fold down and tuck in the sides to create a point.

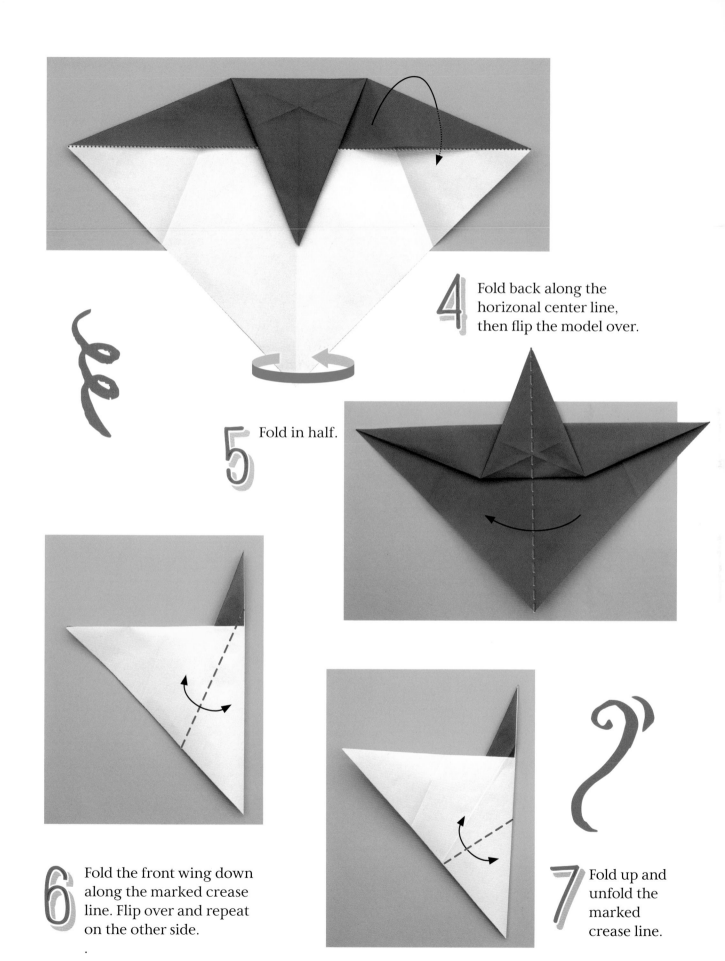

4 Fold back along the horizonal center line, then flip the model over.

5 Fold in half.

6 Fold the front wing down along the marked crease line. Flip over and repeat on the other side.

7 Fold up and unfold the marked crease line.

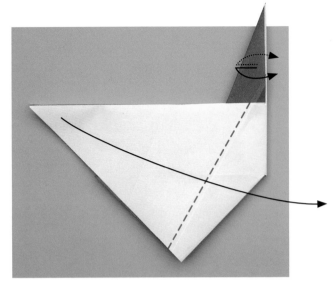

8 Tuck the previous fold up inside the model.

9 Fold down the wing on one side, flip over, and fold down the other wing on the other side. Fold the nose of the plane down as you do this.

10 Fold down the marked crease.

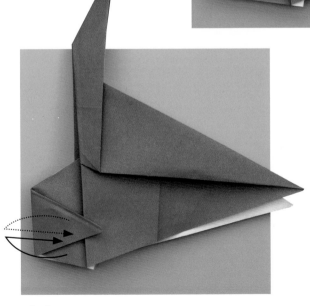

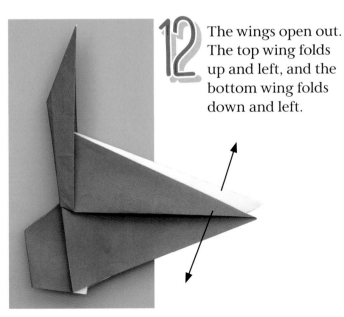

11 Unfold, then tuck inside to create the tail.

12 The wings open out. The top wing folds up and left, and the bottom wing folds down and left.

MARS LANDER

NASA's goal is to send humans to the red planet, Mars, in the 2030s. There are many obstacles to overcome—not least how the astronauts will survive during the months it will take to journey there and back. Landing on Mars will also be a challenge. This module is similar to the one that landed on the Moon.

Start with a single sheet of paper, with the diagonals, and the vertical and horizontal centers creased.

1 Fold the top right corner to the bottom left, and at the same time tuck in the other two corners to make a smaller square. Rotate the square 45 degrees so that the open end is at the bottom.

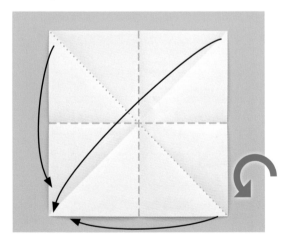

2 Fold in a top edge to the center line.

3 Pull the lower flap out from underneath, then flatten out to open out the fold. Crease and pull it across to the top left edge to make an inverted kite shape.

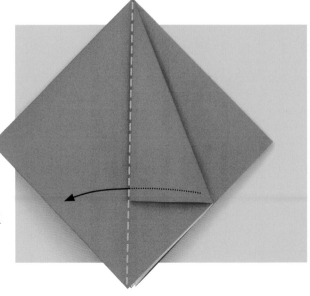

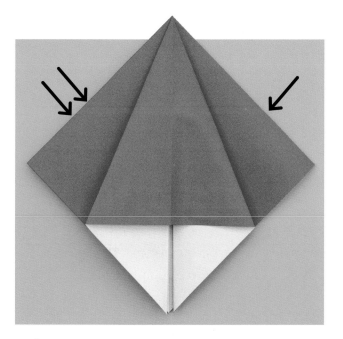

 Repeat steps 2 and 3 three more times with the other flaps.

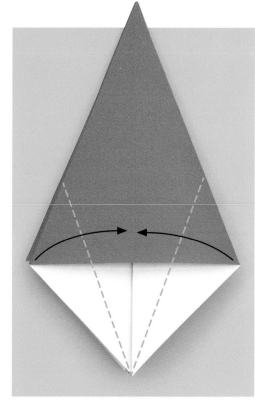

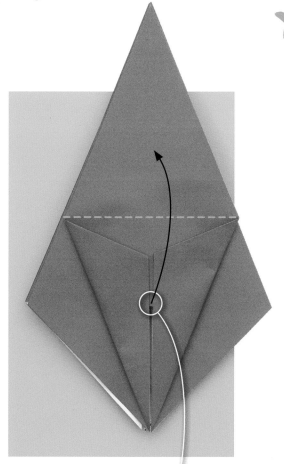

Fold up the bottom edges to the center line.

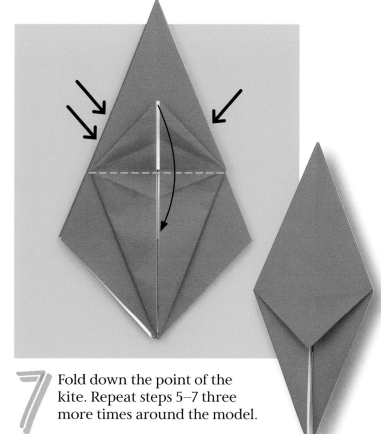

 Pull up the hidden edge and fold it to the center line, making a kite shape.

Fold down the point of the kite. Repeat steps 5–7 three more times around the model.

8 Fold down along the crease line.

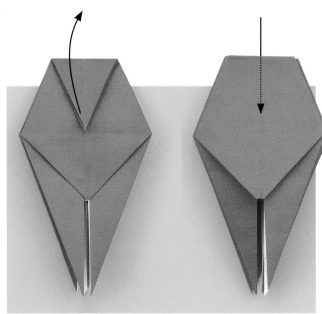

9 Loosely open out the model, then push down the newly folded section into the top of the model so that it is tucked inside. Fold the model flat again.

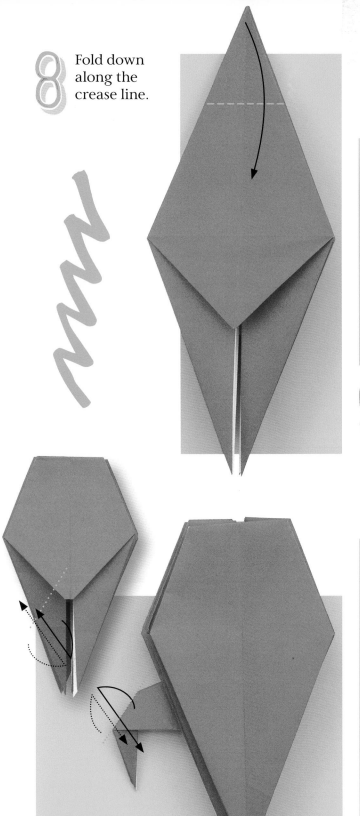

10 Fold up a leg along the crease line. Fold down the knee joint of the leg.

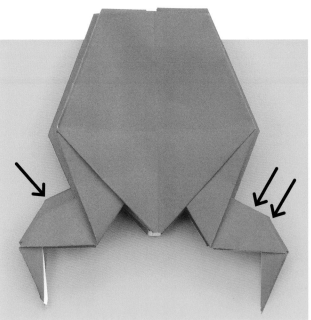

11 Repeat the same process with the remaining three legs.

Open out the model
to complete the
Mars lander.

CANOE

The first canoes were made around 10,000 years ago. The earliest ones were either dugouts made from the trunks of trees, or made of bark on a wooden frame. Modern canoes are made from canvas, aluminum, or plastic.

Start with a sheet of paper, color side up, with a single fold in the middle.

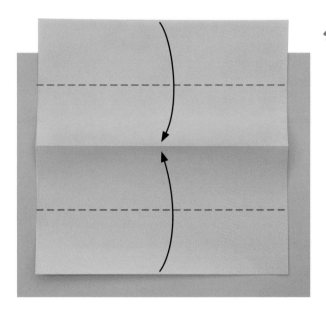

1 Fold the top and bottom edges to the middle.

2 Fold in the four corners as shown.

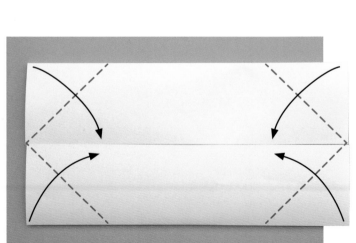

Fold in again along the marked fold lines.

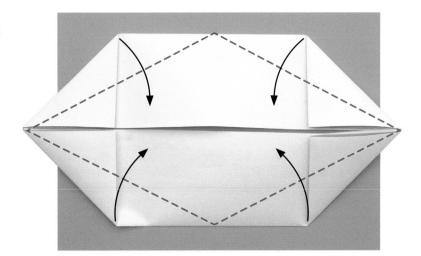

Fold the center top and bottom to the center line.

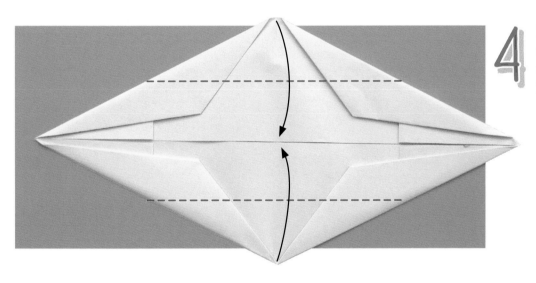

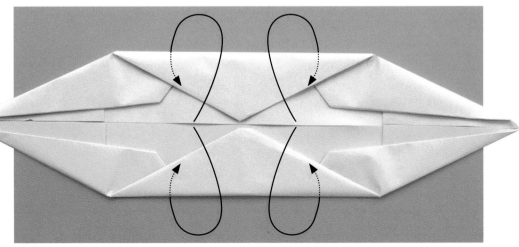
Holding the two middle edges, carefully open out the boat, and turn it inside out to complete the canoe.

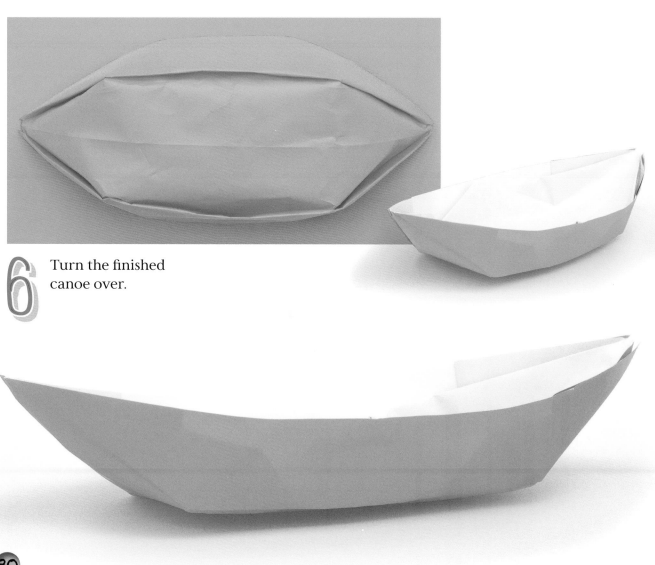

6 Turn the finished canoe over.

DELIVERY VAN

Vans come in many different sizes and are used for transporting goods or people. Small vans are often used for delivering parcels and mail to people's homes. Larger ones are used for moving large items along our roads.

Start with a sheet of paper, face down, with a horizontal center crease.

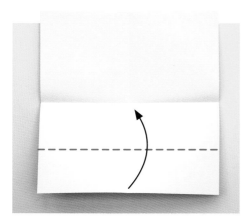

1 Fold up the bottom edge to the center line.

2 Fold down the two diagonals marked.

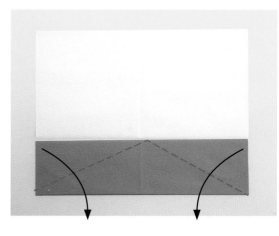

3 Fold the top half down.

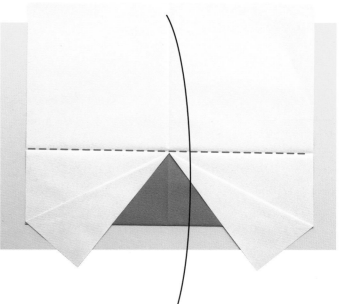

81

4 Fold up the top flap on the crease line.

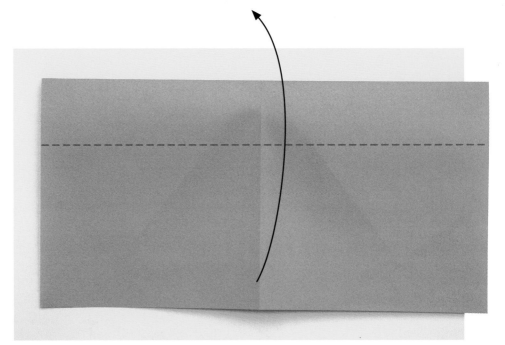

5 Fold in the top right corner along the crease line shown. This will make the front windshield of the van.

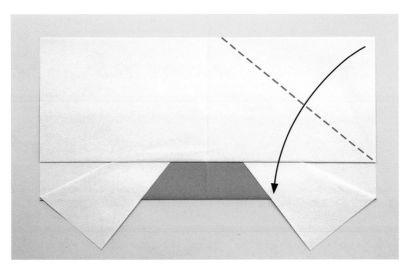

6 Fold up the bottom edges of the tires.

7 Flip the model over to reveal the van!

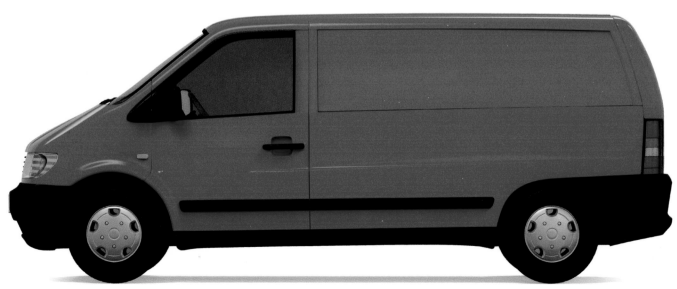

CLASSIC YACHT

Harnessing the wind to glide through the water—sail yachts come in many shapes and sizes. Some superyachts are hundreds of feet long. Yachts are used to race, cross oceans, or just to have fun.

Start with a single sheet, face down, with vertical and horizontal creases.

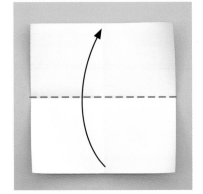

1 Fold up the bottom edge to the top.

2 Fold up the corner to the center line, then unfold.

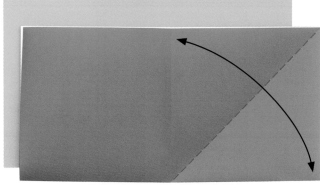

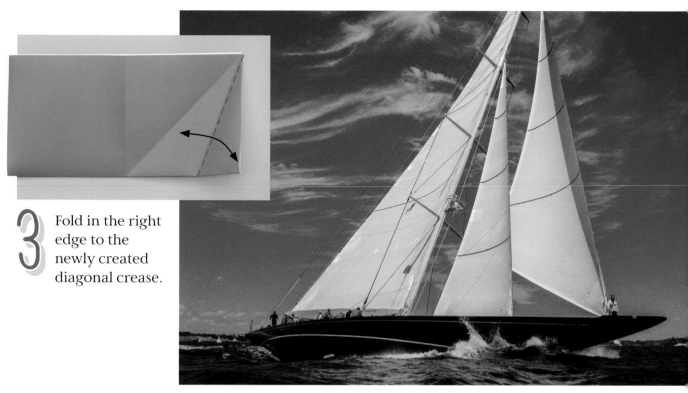

3 Fold in the right edge to the newly created diagonal crease.

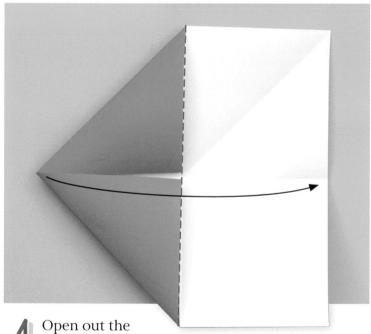

4 Open out the sheet, then fold in the top and bottom corners to the center. Fold in along the vertical center.

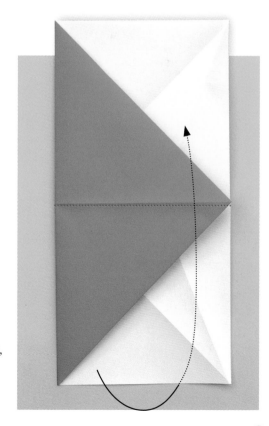

5 Fold under, along the horizontal center.

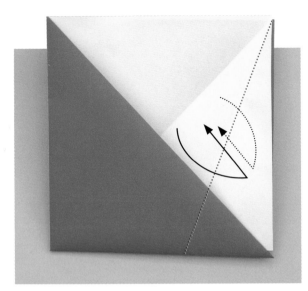

6 Tuck in the front sail along the crease line formed in step 3.

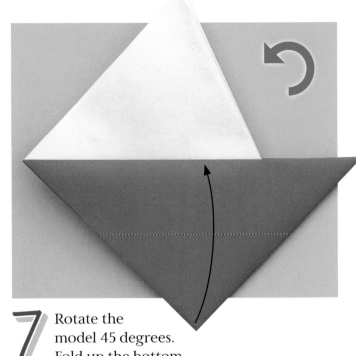

7 Rotate the model 45 degrees. Fold up the bottom corner to the center line.

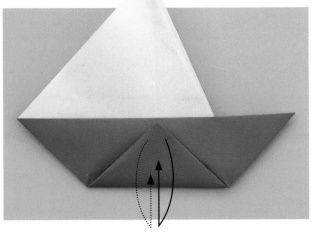

8 Fold and unfold along the crease line shown. Open the boat slightly and tuck the newly creased part up inside, then fold the boat flat to complete the yacht.

SPACE ROCKET

This origami model of a spacecraft is similar to the design of the first Russian space rockets. It is also similar to the rocket used to transport people and goods to the International Space Station.

Start with a single sheet and fold the diagonals, and the vertical and horizontal centers.

1 Fold the top right corner to the bottom left, and at the same time, tuck in the other two corners to make a smaller square. Rotate the square 45 degrees so that the open end is at the bottom.

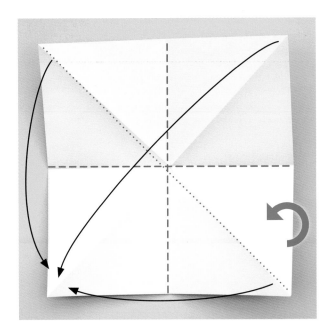

2 Fold in a top edge to the center line.

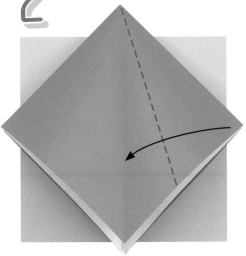

3 Pull out the lower flap from underneath. Then fold back down and flatten out the crease, making an inverted kite shape.

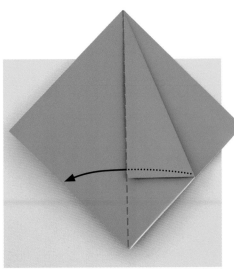

4 Repeat this process three more times with the other flaps.

5 Fold the sides in to the center.

⭐

6 Repeat step 5 with the three other flaps.

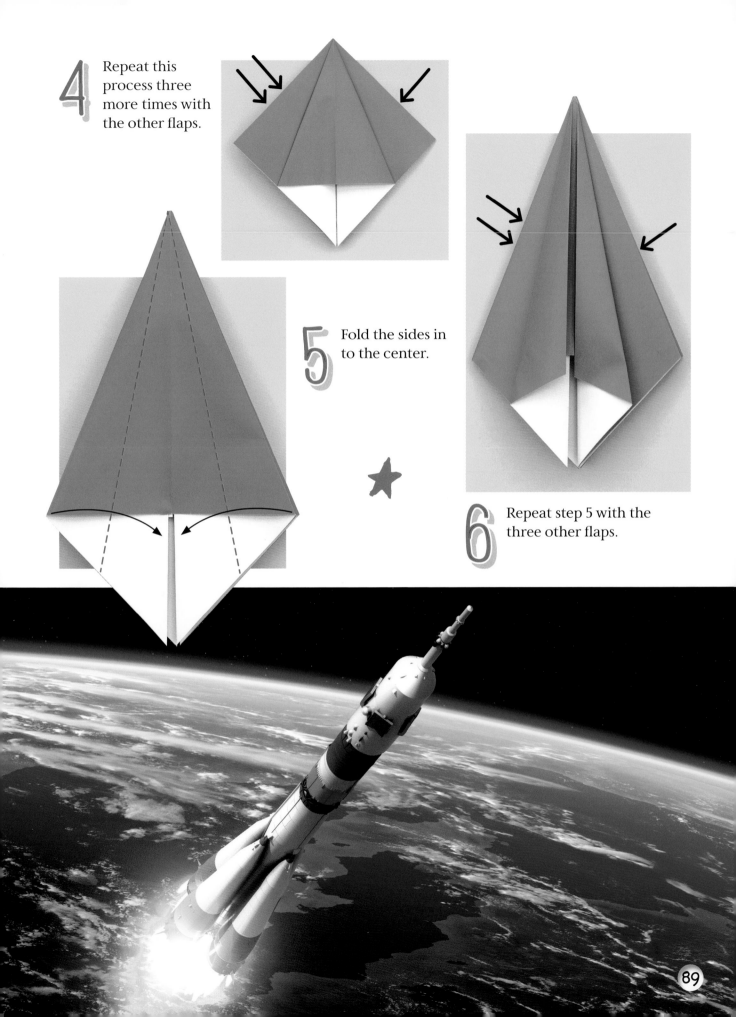

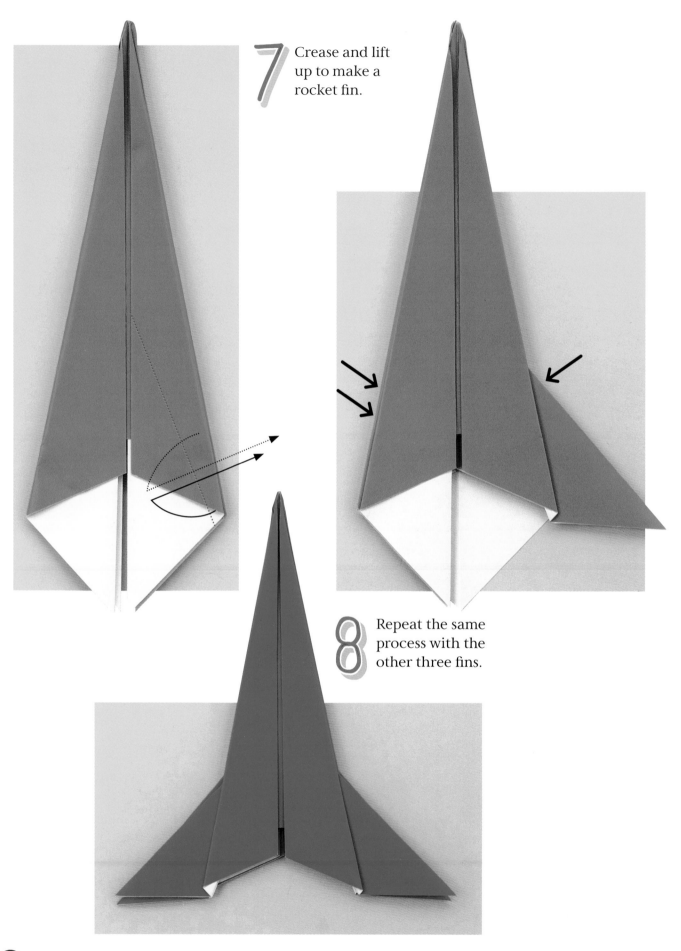

7 Crease and lift up to make a rocket fin.

8 Repeat the same process with the other three fins.

9 Open out the model to
complete the rocket.

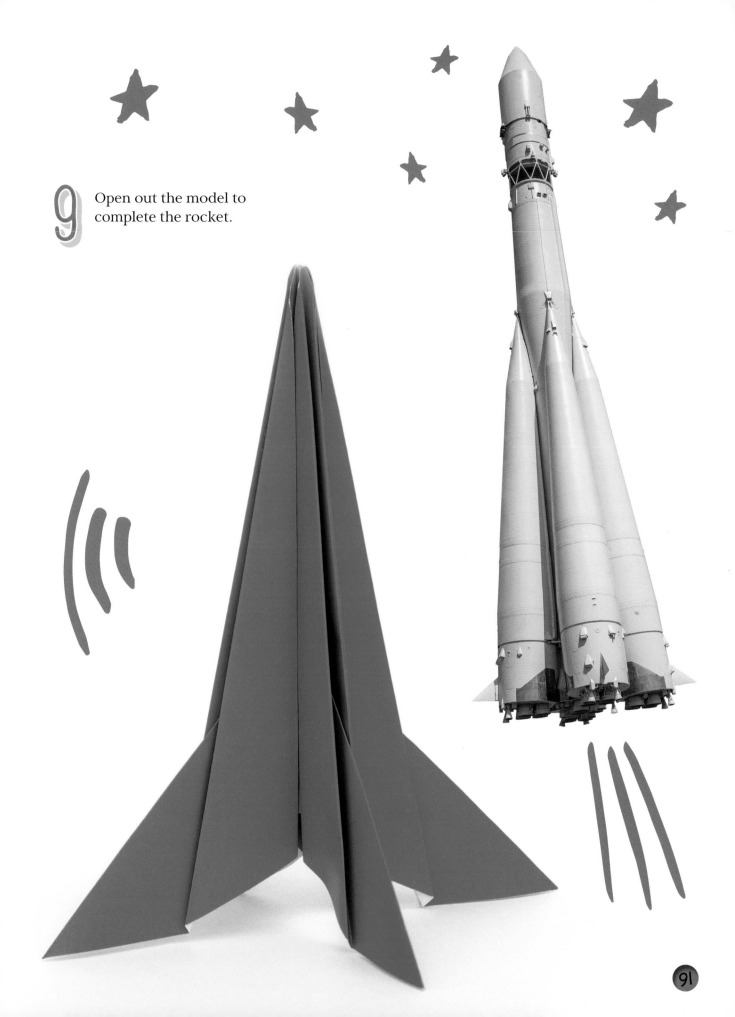

INDEX

Aluminum 78
Apex predator 50
Arm 48
Astronauts 74
Beak 44
Birdwing butterfly 144
Birthday party 68
Buddhist monks 8, 66
Burrows 30
Butterflies 14
Canvas 78
Craft store 9
Concorde 70
Daffodil 54
Dogs 16, 18
Dove of peace 12
Dugouts 78
Eyes 70, 71
Fish 50
Flippers 40
Food chain 36
Foxes 16

Frogs 22
Goliath frog 22
Head 52
Insects 14
International Space Station 78
Japan 8
Japanese crane 8
Jewelry 62
Legs 49, 52
Lucky stars 62
Mammals 26
Mice 26
Moon 74
NASA 74
Neck 52
Nose 48, 51
Reptile 28, 42, 60
Planet Mars 74
Plastic 78
Pencils 66, 67
Pens 64
Poison dart frog 26

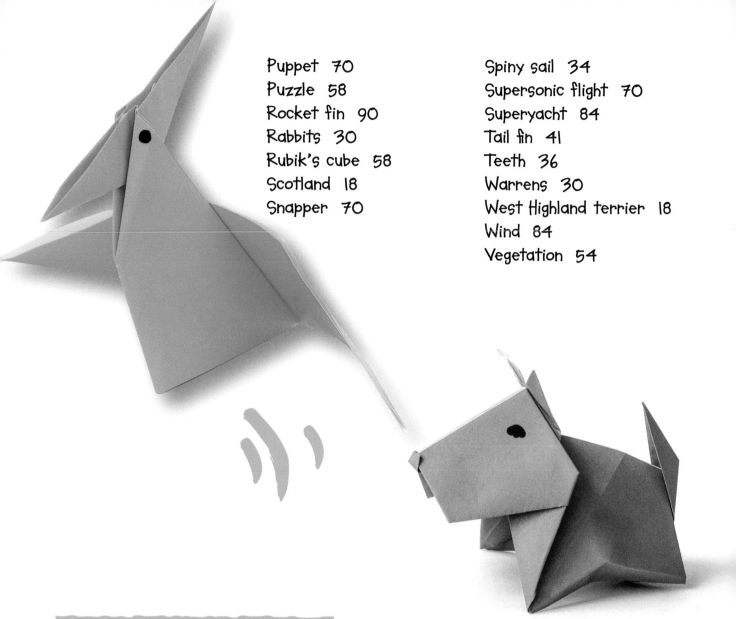

Puppet 70
Puzzle 58
Rocket fin 90
Rabbits 30
Rubik's cube 58
Scotland 18
Snapper 70

Spiny sail 34
Supersonic flight 70
Superyacht 84
Tail fin 41
Teeth 36
Warrens 30
West Highland terrier 18
Wind 84
Vegetation 54

The Author

Rob Ives is a former math and science teacher, now a designer and paper engineer living in Cumbria, UK. He creates science- and project-based children's books, including *Paper Models that Rock!* and *Paper Automata*. He specializes in character-based paper animations and all kinds of fun and fascinating science projects, and often visits schools to talk about design technology and demonstrate his models. Rob's other series for Hungry Tomato include *Tabletop Battles* and *Amazing Science Experiments*.

Picture Credits

(abbreviations: t = top; b = bottom; c = center; l = left; r = right)

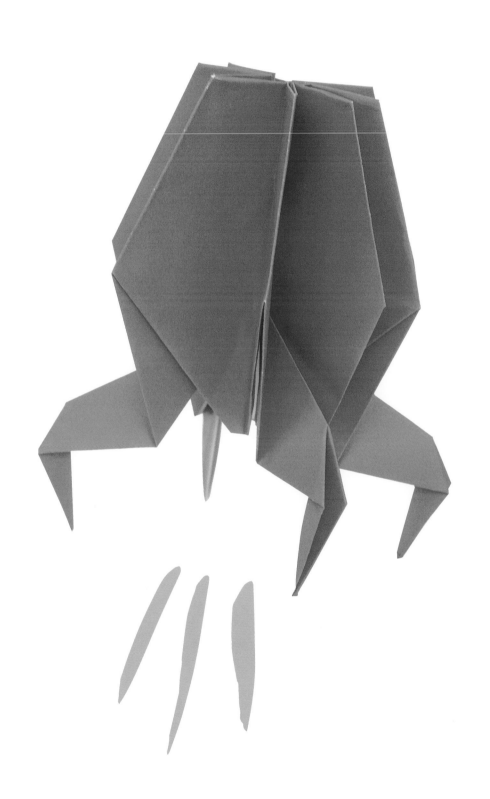

Eek!